Give Me a Child Until He is Seven

Give Me a Child Until He is Seven

Brain Studies and Early Childhood Education

John Brierley

Preface
by

Professor Horace Barlow F.R.S.

 The Falmer Press

(A Member of the Taylor & Francis Group)
London, New York and Philadelphia

UK   The Falmer Press, Falmer House, Barcombe,
            Lewes, East Sussex, BN8 5DL

USA   The Falmer Press, Taylor & Francis Inc., 242
            Cherry Street, Philadelphia, PA 19106–1960

First published 1987
Reprinted 1988

**Library of Congress Cataloging in
Publication Data**

Brierley, John Keith, 1927–
    Give me a child until he is seven.
    1. Learning ability.   2. Child development.
    3. Education, Preschool.   4. Brain—Research.
    I. Title.
    LB1134.B74   1987   372'.21   87–486

    ISBN 1–85000–175–8 (soft)

Typeset in 11/13 Garamond by
Imago Publishing Ltd, Thame, Oxon.

*Printed in Great Britain by
Redwood Burn Limited, Trowbridge, Wiltshire
and bound by Pegasus Bookbinding,
Melksham, Wiltshire.*

Contents

To the many nursery and primary teachers whose experience and expertise provide the solid foundations for much of this book.

Acknowledgements

This book represents the essence of many talks given to parents and to teachers of nursery and infant children, NNEB lecturers, playgroup leaders and teacher trainers over the past twelve years. The comments and constructive criticism after each talk have done much to chasten and improve what is written here for they were based in most instances not on theory but on the reality of the classrooms. The work of many eminent authorities on the brain has been used in writing this book. My contribution has been to draw out of these discoveries some twenty-one principles which seem to me to apply to learning.

Over many years Dr Freda Newcombe, Director of the MRC Neuropsychology Unit at The Radcliffe Infirmary, Oxford and Fellow of Linacre College has given me much help and encouragement with the subject of this book and has also read the typescript. I would like to thank her for her continued interest and beneficial criticism. Professor Horace B Barlow, MD, FRS, Royal Society Research Professor of the Department of Physiology, University of Cambridge, has been generous enough to write an illuminating preface to the book. For this and for his apt advice on the text I thank him. Mrs Rosemary Peacocke, my former HMI colleague, has read the book and given me the benefit of her long experience as a headmistress and teacher of young children and subsequently as Staff Inspector with special responsibility for the education of young children. Professor John Hutt, Professor of Psychology at the University of Keele, has given me much help and encouragement with this subject over many years and I would like to thank him. Mrs Thelma Higgins has patiently and with great care typed the book from my manuscript drafts. My wife, Dr A.F. Brierley, as ever, has read the text and improved it. Any errors of fact and judgment that remain are my own.

J.K. BRIERLEY
December 1986

Preface

The Jesuits' famous saying that is the title of this book expresses a very profound observation, but like so many sweeping statements about the human mind it is an incomplete half-truth. A child's experience up to the age of 7 is enormously important, but we know little about which experiences can benefit a child at an early age, and we are only beginning to understand how they influence the developing brain. Furthermore some individuals surely proceed to change and develop their own beliefs after that age, for if they did not it is unlikely that the religion of the Jesuits would have been created from its seed in Judaism!

What an extraordinarily complicated structure of detailed knowledge awaits discovery behind the half that is true! How are the behaviour, knowledge and beliefs of a 7-year-old child acquired? In this book John Brierley has made a valuable start by explaining why neuroscientists feel optimistic about answering these questions, though no-one should believe that the answers we now give are complete or final. Young animals go through periods in which their brains respond permanently and specifically to particular experiences. For example kittens acquire the capacity for accurate binocular vision and depth discrimination at about five weeks, while puppies acquire the capacity to develop a bond to a human master a few weeks later; for the kittens, the condition for this development is that congruent images of the world should be received simultaneously by the two eyes, while for the pups it is necessary that they should be handled by unthreatening humans before they have been weaned from their mother. There are suggestive parallels with similar age and experience-dependent learning in children, including the almost magical acquisition of language. Investigators of these phenomena in animals are aware of the gulf that separates them from human learning, but surely those interested primarily in humans should pay careful attention to the animal experiments, for it is from them that we shall ultimately learn the all-important details of the processes involved.

There may already be one important practical implication of the results of the experimental approach. The responsibility of bringing up a child is awesome, and parents, as well as teachers, tend to be fearful of the permanent effect of misguided precepts and influences. That is the reason why the second half of the Jesuits' saying '... and he will be mine forever' has rather sinister implications. But so far as they go the animal experiments are somewhat reassuring for they suggest that the greatest harm is done by lack of the appropriate experience at a particular age, rather than by exposure to abnormal experiences. The brain has its own rhythm of development, and the influence of experience seems to be more *permissive* than *instructive*. It is as if the infant brain develops to a point when it can profit from an experience, and if this happens it goes ahead to the next stage, but if it misses the experience it cannot proceed along that path and finds another. Development is to some extent self-correcting, so that a faulty step does not seem to be as serious as one might fear; the child who is taught an incorrect meaning for a word quite rapidly ceases to use it because he finds that it does not work in the way he expects, and the brain may be able to minimize the wrong effects of its experiences in a similar way.

If mental and moral development in humans follows the crude animal models we have so far, the fear that we do not provide enough intellectual stimulus to the developing mind has more justification than the fear that it will be warped by unsuitable experience. Perhaps one should now replace the Jesuit boast with the more liberal statement 'If you do not ensure that children undergo certain experiences by the age of 7, they will have lost forever the chance of benefitting from them'. In the present state of knowledge this is speculation, but it illustrates the importance of understanding the mechanisms involved in much greater detail than we do now.

Beyond the astute remark made more than four centuries ago lies a wealth of detailed knowledge that can only be uncovered by painstaking scientific experiments. This book describes the first few steps on this path, and perhaps already allows us to see the facts of early mental development from a slightly different viewpoint. No one should doubt that there is much more to discover from animals before we can reasonably claim to know how experience influences the mind of a child, and the advances waiting to be made are likely to have a profound influence on enlightened educational practice.

Horace Barlow MD ScD FRS
Royal Society Research Professor of Physiology
Physiological Laboratory Cambridge.

1   Introduction

Many parents, and indeed most experienced teachers, marvel at the miracle of progress a child makes in his two or three years in the infant school. By comparison with a child of 5 a normal child at the end of the infant stage is capable of assuming responsibility and exercising leadership. He will have acquired a measure of social discipline and he can be expected to be friendly, lively and responsive. Unless he is very slow he will have advanced a long way and in many directions in his work. He will have made a satisfactory start in learning to read, write and calculate. His memory and imagination are good. He can express himself often very well in talk and through writing. Indeed, linguistic ability seems to accelerate in many children towards the end of the seventh year when the quality and quantity of what they say and write about never fails to surprise and delight. Children at this stage have learnt to use many different kinds of material for work in art and craft. Hand and eye coordination are quite good and their paintings in particular often have a freshness and directness which is never regained. They can use their physical powers with confidence and their bodies with increasing dexterity and enjoyment. But even before the start of formal schooling at five any parent or nursery teacher will recognize how developed are his curiosity, critical sense and imagination.

In 1972 a Government White Paper, *A Framework for Expansion*[1], devoted a section to the under-5s and stated:

> We now know that, given sympathetic and skilled supervision, children may be able to make educational progress before the age of 5. They are capable of developing further in the use of language, in thought and in practical skills than was previously supposed.

Unfortunately the impetus for the expansion of pre-school provision witnessed in the 1970s has been lost and education has failed to capitalize on a period in human development when the brain and sense organs are highly developed and the capacity to learn is at flood-readiness.

My two chief aims in this short book are to use evidence from brain studies to demonstrate the young brain's potential, flexibility and resilience and especially to highlight the crucial importance of the pre-school and early school years. What is known lends support for more and better opportunities for children in these vital years of life from birth to about 8.

Throughout the book I have ventured to underscore some principles for the education of young children at school and in playgroups arising from brain studies. Some of these will apply to older children as well. For ease of reference I have collected these principles together in Chapter 12.

Important discoveries from brain science arise from many directions but the pieces of research lie scattered like a jigsaw puzzle half finished and no overall picture of how the brain works is yet in sight. Indeed knowledge of the overall action of the brain has been less touched by science than by anything else that influences our daily lives to the same degree.[2] This is not surprising. The brain is delicate, complex and hidden and its fine structure is fantastically intricate. Anatomical work on brain structure is immensely laborious and needs courage, persistence and good technical support to carry it through. For our purposes in attempting to relate the physical brain to higher mental functions a degree of modesty is required in the use of the evidence.

Much of what *is* known about the brain supports the common sense and instincts of the vast majority of parents and teachers and the more insights that are gained from what is known the more our motives are strengthened towards providing a good environment for learning at home and school. As I hope to show, a good environment is not a luxury but a necessity during the early years of life. It is important to know that it is good to talk to a child, that young children need to play and explore, that experience of touch, sound and sight are vital, that memory and imagination are important for development, that a broad curriculum which teaches a child to notice and to think is crucial and that a secure family life with the affectionate care of adults whom a child can trust and who can set him standards are essential. The reason *why* all this should be so provides essential depth to this knowledge and strengthens the motives for planning good opportunities. Only a part of this background can be added by brain studies but it is important to possess it, not only to enhance development, but to prevent injustices arising.

Notes

1 HMSO (1972)
2 PHILLIPS, C.G. *et al* (1984) 'Localisation of function in the cerebral cortex', *Brain*, 107

2   *The Brain*

The brain of a normal adult weighs about three pounds. Passingham[1] has made an interesting deduction: that the human brain is three times as large as would be expected in a hypothetical primate of our build. Though large it is not simply a bigger version of an ape's brain; rather those parts concerned with learning, the cerebellum and cortex (see diagram), are developed to about three times the size of those in, say, a chimpanzee. The cerebellum ensures steady, skilful and properly timed movements under the overall control of the cortex which itself is largely concerned with thinking, planning, hearing, speaking and seeing. As befits its vital role as the human thinking cap, the cortex is about half the weight of the entire nervous system.

Another instructive fact is that the size of the brain and head show an astonishing range of individual variation. Although on average the brain weighs about three pounds, about 1350 grammes, the variation in weight of the large majority of men's brains lies between 1180 and 1704 grammes and all but 5 per cent of women have a range in brain weight which lies between 1033 and 1533 grammes (women are smaller anyway). Despite this vast variation it has not been possible to relate differences in weight to differences in intellectual ability except in instances where brain weight is well below the normal range. The cut off point for normality in adults seems to lie below 1000 grammes.

Karl Pearson[2] eighty years ago made measurements of head size and academic performance in over 1000 students and 12-year-old boys and girls and obtained correlations between head measurements and academic performance 'so small that they are in every case of no service for the purposes of prediction'. Subsequent work has confirmed Pearson's view. It seems then that the main asset of a brilliant child is not more grey matter but that he/she somehow or other has a knack of using the ordinary brain machinery differently. This does not rule out the distinct possibility that the brain of a particular child possesses unique features that cannot readily be detected by the microscope.

Brain surgeons, when looking at a living brain, say that its strangest quality is its stillness, giving no hint of character or ability. The fact that nerves run to it from all over the body and away from it indicates that it has overall control. Though it is one organ it consists of four closely interlinked parts: the cortex (grey matter); the brain stem whose upper part forms the central core of the brain (sometimes called the 'old' brain, old in the evolutionary sense); the lower brain stem or 'bulb' and the cerebellum (see diagram).

Cortex

It is with the cortex that I shall be primarily concerned because it plays a major role in learning, thinking and planning and further details about it will be picked up and elaborated in later chapters.

The cortex lies on the outer surface of the brain and is a mantle of about 2000 cms^2 in area, immensely folded to pack its enormous area into the skull. The sheet of cortex is about 3 mm thick and is formed from nerve cells (neurones) of many varieties and sizes, in all about 10,000 million. This

Diagram 1

Side view of the human brain. Adapted from UNESCO *Courier* January 1976.
Dotted area = bulb or lower brain stem. Hatched area = 'old' brain or upper brain stem.

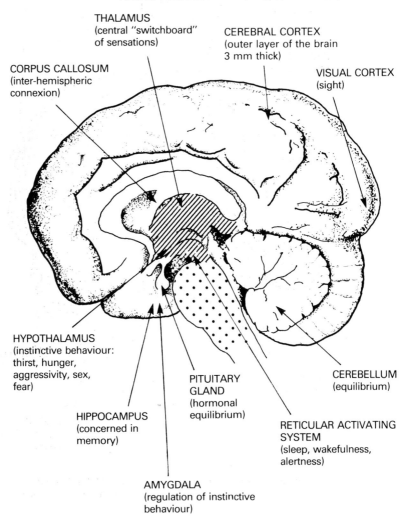

RIGHT HEMISPHERE (inside)

THALAMUS
(central "switchboard"
of sensations)

CEREBRAL CORTEX
(outer layer of the brain
3 mm thick)

CORPUS CALLOSUM
(inter-hemispheric
connexion)

VISUAL CORTEX
(sight)

HYPOTHALAMUS
(instinctive behaviour:
thirst, hunger,
aggressivity, sex,
fear)

PITUITARY
GLAND
(hormonal
equilibrium)

CEREBELLUM
(equilibrium)

HIPPOCAMPUS
(concerned in
memory)

RETICULAR ACTIVATING
SYSTEM
(sleep, wakefulness,
alertness)

AMYGDALA
(regulation of instinctive
behaviour)

LEFT HEMISPHERE (outside)

SENSORY CORTEX
(body sensations)

OCCIPITAL LOBE
(sight)

MOTOR CORTEX
(body movements)

PARIETAL LOBE
(seems to control relationship
between body and mind.
Injuries may distort "body image")

FRONTAL LOBE
(decision making)

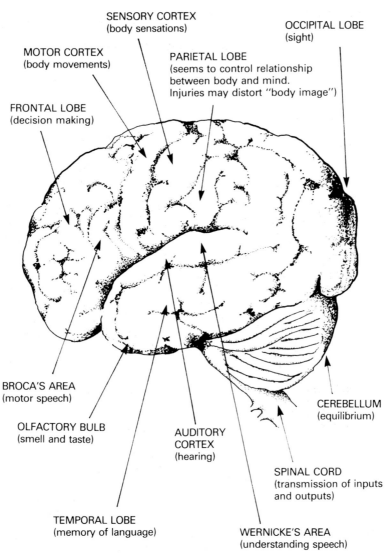

BROCA'S AREA
(motor speech)

OLFACTORY BULB
(smell and taste)

AUDITORY
CORTEX
(hearing)

CEREBELLUM
(equilibrium)

SPINAL CORD
(transmission of inputs
and outputs)

TEMPORAL LOBE
(memory of language)

WERNICKE'S AREA
(understanding speech)

7

rough estimate has been made by counting the neurones and multiplying up.

When sections of cortex from a variety of mammals are examined under a microscope the number of cells in comparable sections of the same size is, remarkably, similar in all mammals. This rather startling fact is because the lower density in large brained animals such as ourselves is compensated for by an increase in depth of cortex. The spacing of neurones may be of special importance because the less densely they are packed the greater the number of nerve pathways that can be made between them; and, though it is a speculation, the richness and variety of branching and connectivity may be important in the development of intelligence. The spacing of neurones in the human cortex would facilitate this.

Beneath the top rind of the grey matter of the cortex (grey because it contains the cell bodies of the neurones) the bulk of the tissue is a pulpy white matter formed from million upon million of criss-crossing fibres (axons) of the neurones conducting nerve impulses. A record from the surface of the brain would show electrical oscillations taking place all the time due to groups of neurones continually discharging electrical signals. Though the number of neurones is vast in the cortex, they are found in other parts of the brain as well. The cerebellum contains millions itself. Despite the staggering number of neurones, they are, surprisingly, in a small minority among brain cells as a whole and about 80 per cent of brain weight is due to glial cells.[3] The purpose of these numerous cells is a mystery. They may serve as packing material to the delicate neurones but nature is less wasteful than this. Their close relationship to the surfaces of the neurones could suggest that they may play a part in nourishing the latter and perhaps also in the specific function of nerve conduction. Some recent suggestions are that they may be concerned with memory.

All the cells in the brain might add up to 100,000

million packed into the smallish space of our head. The vastness of this number of cells, what they do and how they connect so that we achieve a unity of thought, is as paralyzing to our understanding as the vastness of space.

Embedded in the pulpy white matter under the cortex are some solid masses of grey matter of various kinds and I shall return to these in a moment.

Perhaps rather surprisingly, the cortex is divided into two distinct halves, the left and right hemispheres, each with different functional roles. The left is more concerned with speech and the programming of skilled movements and the right with some visuospatial skills, such as recognizing faces and reading maps. While the hemispheres do have different domains of specialization, pushing the contrast between them too far would be misleading.[4] The right hemisphere has some limited verbal comprehension. It is better at concrete rather than abstract words, and in those rare cases of children whose left hemisphere has had to be removed because of disease or injury before age 2, clear simple speech develops in the right. Similarly the left hemisphere also contributes to face recognition both in the healthy adult and in the infant whose right hemisphere has had to be removed.

The two hemispheres are connected by a tough strap of nerves, the corpus callosum, which enables them to work together as a balanced system. At any one time it is as though one pan of the scales, so to speak, is raised, while the other is lowered to give harmony to thinking and behaviour. It is unknown how this mental unity is achieved or in what form information is transmitted from one hemisphere to another.

The Four Lobes

Each hemisphere has four lobes on it: temporal, occipital, parietal and frontal (see diagram). The temporal lobe is like the thumb of a boxing glove when the fist is clenched.

Tucked inside each is a twisted structure shaped like a sea-horse and hence called the hippocampus. Certain parts of the temporal lobes and their associated hippocampi play a crucial part in learning and memory.[5]

Parts of the cortex are specialized respectively for hearing, sight, taste, smell and touch and also for physical movement (the 'motor' area) and most function from birth. If any of these 'primary' areas is destroyed by accident or injury, the sense or function is lost. If the primary visual area in the occipital lobe at the back of the cortex is wholly destroyed — a rare occurrence — blindness results.

Adjacent to the primary areas are large regions of the cortex vital to specific aspects of memory and learning. These 'association' areas occupy the large frontal part of the cortex, large parts of the sides (the parietal areas) and the temporal lobes but their exact function is difficult to pin down. They are currently thought to specialize in the processing and storage of 'modality-specific' information (ie, specific to a particular sensory channel such as vision, hearing, taste, smell, movement and so on). Thus damage to the left temporal lobe selectively impairs the learning and retention of words and letters. Conversely damage to the right leaves verbal memory intact but disturbs the recognition of visual and auditory patterns — tunes, places, faces — that do not lend themselves to verbal coding. Injury to the parietal lobes can cause strange disturbances of the relationship between body and mind such as loss of consciousness of the existence of the right side of the body if the left parietal lobe is injured so that the affected person may only shave half his face or comb half his hair. In an everyday sense the parietal region may account for the amazing accomplishments of spatial orientation; the ability to find one's way home, dress oneself and, perhaps in association with other parts of the cortex, even preserve a sense of bodily existence.

The much enlarged frontal lobes, whose nature is poorly understood, do not appear to be a homogeneous region but show considerable specialization of function. They perhaps give us the capacity to cooperate with others, to restrain aggressive and sexual capacities, to think things out and judge the consequences of our actions. The frontal lobes are in close communication with the other association areas and other deeper parts of the brain.

It is on these differently specialized association areas that memory and learning largely depend and consequently our intelligent understanding and use of the world. Memory will be discussed in chapter 10 but it may be noted in passing that memory is not a passive structure but is part of an action system[6] which allows us to think and predict on the basis of sensory information.

The way that the two hemispheres are linked to the body is a remarkable and strange feature of the nervous system. The nerve connections are primarily 'contralateral' (opposite side) rather than 'ipsilateral' (same side). This means that the movement and sensation of the left side of the body is controlled mainly by the right hemisphere and the right side of the body by the left hemisphere. When a person picks up his pen with his left hand the sensory information detailing the shape and texture of the pen travels largely to the right hemisphere. We can actually describe it in words because information in the right hemisphere travels across the nerve bridge (corpus callosum) mentioned earlier, to the left hemisphere.

Brain Maps

Part of the cortex can be justly compared with spatial maps because the nerve fibres bringing signals from the sense organs are arranged on the cortex in a regular pattern which precisely represents every point of the receptive surface of the body — skin or the retina of the eye — in correct relationship with its neighbours. There is a whole detailed atlas of sequential maps for vision, a less detailed one (not yet established) for hearing (chapter 6) while touch is well charted. No detailed maps exist for smell or taste but there is an excellent map for muscles on the motor area of the cortex already mentioned. It is not clear whether these maps are static or plastic but it is clear that there are profound differences between them.

The motor area of the cortex is a strip of brain tissue on each side of it. It can be traced in the head from the crown downwards and forwards to a point a little above and in front of the ear. The map is of the muscles on the opposite side of the body as already indicated, but it is a curiously distorted map[7] with more than half of it devoted to the hands and the speech organs. To add a detail, about six times more grey matter is made over to the lips than to the whole trunk. This distortion is merely a reflection of the importance of speech and of the hands in our daily lives.

Behind the motor cortex is a second strip that represents a touch map of the entire body surface from the sense organs in the skin (see diagram). Again, it is distorted with over representation of the face and hands. The underlying principle of these two brain maps seems to be that the most important areas of the body are most generously represented on the map.

Much is known about visual maps. There are a dozen or more in the monkey and presumably in man, and more may turn up yet. Before looking at this amazing atlas of vision in a bit more detail, it is worth mentioning that what is sent to the brain from a sense organ like the eye or the skin is not an accurate copy of a scene or object handled but a simplified electrical and chemical code which specific parts of the brain cortex interprets as sight or touch.

It is not known how the brain classifies and combines these electrical and chemical signals into integrated forms but, returning to vision, experiments with animals show that there are cells in the visual cortex which respond electrically, that is 'fire', to the stimulus of a whole range of shapes: slits, lines, corner shapes, colour, movement and even paw and face shapes.

The analysis of separate features like these seems to be the first step by the brain in the summation of the parts of a scene into larger wholes. The cells of the visual cortex are arranged in their millions with crystalline regularity. Cells are organized in columns and each appears to be a machine equipped to analyze the visual events that occur in a minute part of each retina of the eye.

It is unlikely that the visual maps in the human brain have highly specific groups of cells adapted to recognize one particular face or situation, though perhaps lips curled into a smile is one. There are, however, a large number of inter-linked visual areas[8] on the cortex, the atlas referred to, each concerned with the interpretation of different aspects of the visual world — colour, orientation, depth, motion and texture. One, the primary visual cortex at the back of the brain, perhaps analyzes local features of an image sent from the eyes and serves to relay specific feature attributes of it for further higher order analysis and interpretation by the specialized visual areas mentioned.

The generalized properties of these feature-detecting cells rather than highly specific ones 'pre-set' to detect a hand, face or tree, lend weight to the basic notion of the open, flexible brain. Nevertheless, although remarkable advances have been made into this bewildering visual terri-tory in the last ten years, exactly where and how patterns of visual impressions unite to form fully integrated images in our consciousness with simultaneously or temporally dis-tinct patterns of other sensory impressions 'is a mystery'. Zuckermann[9] expressed this view thirty-five years ago and the position has not changed much.

Though we do not yet know *how* the brain achieves this marvellous feat we do have a good idea of *where* it does it through the work of the brain surgeon Wilder Penfield.

Penfield drew up a map of the functions of the cortex by observing the results of gentle electrical stimulation of the surface of the cortex exposed during brain operations on human patients. The surgery was performed under local anaesthetic and so the patient was awake to report on conscious sensations created by the stimulations. Electrical 'tickling' of some areas of the visual cortex (which is not painful) made the patient see swirling coloured shapes. These shapes were perceived as somewhere in front of the patient's eyes and not in the head. Stimulation of parts of the temporal cortex sometimes caused patients to have 'flashbacks' of whole moving scenes, which included voices.

It seems possible, therefore, that specific sites on the temporal lobes are concerned with the final summation and storage of the relatively simple feature analyses carried out in the complex series of maps referred to.[10]

Despite our present knowledge the cortex as a whole is still rather like an old map with only the gross landmarks known but there is cause for optimism among experts. Within a few years it is very likely that some of the elusive secrets of the cortex will be understood because of improved techniques for investigating brain structure. The range of known facts about the cortex does allow useful speculations to be made about how it works. This in turn allows new approaches to be explored, old ideas to be discounted and new ones pursued, always with the knowledge 'that the one certain thing about the future of brain studies is that there will be surprises which will alter radically our way of thinking about the brain'[11].

The Automatic Pilot

The cerebellum, or little brain, lies below the back of the cortex and is second only to the cortex in size. It is corrugated by deep side to side ridges which increase its surface area. It is really an enormous computer to organize body movements. Perhaps a better description of it is 'an automatic pilot'. It takes over actions merely sketched out by our conscious minds and arranges complex muscle teamwork to bring actions about such as walking, reaching, picking up things accurately and learned skills like handwriting. If the cerebellum goes wrong the cortex itself must carry out the detailed arrangements of the muscles. Actions can still be carried out but they are slow, unsure, tiring and inaccurate[12].

The 'Old' Brain

The 'old' brain lies deep in the middle of the skull overlain by the great convoluted cortex. This area contains a number of interlinked structures embodied in the pulpy white matter mentioned earlier, which seem to provide the springs of life urging us to act and feel as we do. One of these is the thalamus, which is a relay station for sensory messages to the cerebral cortex. There is some evidence that it adds emotional drive to cortical activities that otherwise might be colourless — a sunset and a rainbow give delight. It also re-sorts signals from the sense organs into new patterns which are projected onto the maps for vision, hearing and touch already referred to.

Below the thalamus is the hypothalamus, about as big as a damson, pressed against the floor of the skull and surrounded by nerves, blood vessels and glands. For all its small size it is the supreme regulator of the internal organs of the body (such as stomach and intestines) through the autonomic (or involuntary) nervous system which regulates bodily activities not entirely under the will and also of the pituitary gland which lies below it and which produces many hormones that regulate slow processes such as growth and reproduction. Again there is a link between the cortex and old brain, as in the thalamus. If you worry in your cortex, the hypothalamus knows and alerts the autonomic system.

The hypothalamus contains numerous 'centres' for regulating temperature and such activities as eating, drinking and sexual rhythms.

Despite the remarkable properties of the cortex it would be a lifeless machine without the power supply of the reticular formation, a complex, untidy tangle of nerve fibres running up and down near the centre of the brain and responsible for attention, sleep and wakefulness. The link between the cortex and the mid-brain is once more illustrated because consciousness itself is dependent on the activity of the reticular formation acting in conjunction with the cortex.

The precise relationship of the thalamus and hypothalamus and other structures in the old brain to our subjective feelings is very difficult to decide, but there is little doubt that most of our desires and even conscious decisions are at least strongly influenced by these deep brain structures. In children who have not learned to school their emotions as well as adults, this part of the brain often gains control and so a 5-year-old can experience undiluted rage, fear, fun, delight and sadness. In much older children and adults the fierce irrationality between what we feel and 'know in our mind to be best' is commonplace.

The Bulb

Finally there is the bulb, the lower part of the brain stem which continues the spinal cord into the skull. In it are centres for the control of life and death functions like breathing and the maintenance of temperature control.

In this brief description of the brain I have somewhat compartmentalized it. But it does not work in sections. There are probably no set areas responsible for higher thinking like problem-solving or painting pictures. Though it has specialized areas the brain seems to work as one unit and thinking and feeling go on throughout the brain whenever necessary.

The Fuel of the Brain

For all its amazing work the brain is simple in its fuel requirements. The fuels for our thoughts are glucose and oxygen and the brain's need for these two simple substances is continuous and avid. Oxygen is consumed by the adult brain at about 46 cm^3 per hour which is one-quarter of the total oxygen used by the resting body, but individual parts — the visual cortex — when functioning use oxygen at a greater rate than other parts. Glucose, mostly converted from other foods, is used by adults at the rate of 108 grammes a day. The breakdown of glucose by oxygen yields energy, about twenty watts per unit time, the electricity supply necessary to light a dim bulb. Eating more sugar or breathing more oxygen will not improve the quality of our thinking any more than putting more current through a TV set will improve its performance. If carbon dioxide, a bi-product of sugar breakdown and energy release, is not shifted away from the brain by the circulation, it soon falters, choked as it were by its own smoke.

The Open, Flexible Brain

Many principles for teaching and learning emerge from this brief account of the brain. I will draw out the first. *Most of the cortex at birth is like a blank slate on which the lessons of experience will be written, including those of language. The nature of the slate is of course determined by heredity.* The parts of the cortex involved are the association areas, in particular the temporal and frontal lobes. A child focussing his attention on something that takes his interest learns. What he learns is written on the slate or, to change the metaphor, blazes a trail through the thicket of nerve connections in the cortex. The quality of experience a child receives is vital for the sound development of the brain's blank areas. There is a price to be paid for this remarkable plasticity because if children are educationally, socially and culturally disadvantaged they may suffer impairments not necessarily by altering nerve pathways, though this is quite possible but by creating within them a poor state of mind and low self-esteem.

The notion of large areas of the cortex as a blank slate is simple and rather misleading. The potential for the development of the association areas is to some extent determined by heredity so that one person's abilities will differ from another's given the same experiences. As a child grows he is formed gradually by the imprint of experience interacting with heredity. In this way the brain develops, strengthening its powers by practice rather like a muscle. These dynamic properties are quite unlike those of a passive slate. Nevertheless none of this undermines the basic openness and flexibility of the young brain which within limits set by heredity is subject to alteration by teaching and the personal effort a child makes himself.

Notes

1 PASSINGHAM, D. (1982) *The Human Primate*, W.H. Freeman
2 HARRIS, J.L. (1985) cited in 'Delicacy of fibres in the brain ...' in GHESQUIERE, R.D., MARTIN, R.D. and NEWCOMBE, F. (Eds) *Human Sexual Dimorphism*, Taylor & Francis
3 DOBBING, J. (1984) 'Infant nutrition and later achievement', *Nutrition Reviews*, 42, 1
4 MILNER, B. (1971) 'Interhemispheric differences in the localisation of psychological processes in man', *British Medical Bulletin*, 27, 3

5 PENFIELD, W. (1981) *The Mystery of the Mind*, Princeton
6 YOUNG, J.Z. (1978) *Programs of the Brain*, Oxford University Press
7 PENFIELD, W. and ROBERTS, L. (1959) *Speech and Brain Mechanisms*, Princeton
8 BARLOW, H.B. (1981) 'Critical limiting factors in the design of the eye and visual cortex', *Proceedings of the Royal Society*
9 ZUCKERMAN, S. (1950) 'The mechanism of thought' in LASLETT, P. (Ed) *The Physical Basis of Mind*, Blackwell
10 FRISBY, J.P. (1979) *Seeing*, Oxford University Press
11 PHILLIPS, C.G. *et al.* (1984) 'Localisation of function in the cerebral cortex', *Brain*. 107.
12 ELLIOT, H.C. (1970) *The Shape of Intelligence*, Allen & Unwin

3   Habits and Skills

It is time for some detail about the key component of the brain and nervous system, the neurone. It has been estimated that there are ten billion nerve cells in the brain, each capable of developing its own electrical charge. Wilder Penfield, the brain surgeon previously mentioned, observed that the brain 'vibrates' with an energy that in health is held in disciplined control. Conduction of nerve signals is facilitated by the shape of the neurones which can be simple or complex. From the main cell body sprouts a single axon, essentially a long wire covered with white insulation, the white pulpy matter of the brain mentioned earlier. The axon carries the nerve impulses, not as a continual stream of electricity like water through a pipe, but as a series of impulses like bullets from a machine gun. Almost all, if not all, neurones are spontaneously active, 'firing' (discharging an electrical impulse) as often as ten times a second. Any message they transmit has to be an increase or decrease in this spontaneous base-line rate of discharge.

From the main cell body other shorter branches extend. These are the dendrites which may be few or many and simply or profusely branched. They receive messages from sense organs like the eye, skin or ear or, in most cases from other neurones. These messages may be of different kinds and a given neurone combines or 'sums' the impulses it picks up through its dendrites. On the basis of this information a neurone increases or decreases the rate at which it produces pulses of electricity. At the end of the axon the pulses of electricity cause a flow of chemicals to be released which cross the gap between neurones to stimulate or inhibit the next neurone in the chain. Thus a message, electrical and chemical in nature, is passed along a chain of neurones, or perhaps rather a web than a chain. The sub-microscopic gap between two neurones is the synapse which acts as a kind of valve forcing impulses to flow in one direction so that messages do not meet head on. The synapse seems to act as a super filter sorting important messages from trivial ones and merging simple messages into complex blends. There may be as many as 20,000 synapses on the dendrites of one large cortical neurone and 2000 on a smaller one.

Each neurone is linked by synapses to other neurones, in some cases it seems to be as many as a quarter of a million. When a nerve pathway is much used, the 'threshold' of the synapse falls so that it operates more readily. An impulse discharged from one neurone causes a momentary activation (or inhibition) in the synapses which each neurone forms with other neurones but for an effective spread of activity each neurone must receive synaptic bombardment from hundreds of thousands of neurones and itself transmit to thousands of others. Thus a wave front of activity is started which might sweep over at least 100,000 neurones in a second. An advancing wave would also branch at intervals, often abortively and join with other waves, to give a complex and fleeting pattern. The impulse down a nerve depends not only on electrical but also on chemical energy and this driving power is derived from the simple substances mentioned in the last chapter.

Stimulus-response Memory

Several aspects of nerve function are important to highlight in the context of teaching and learning. One is the fundamental tendency for nerve cells to repeat patterns of activity that have once occurred and around which more elaborate responses can be built.[1] During the height of the response the nerve cells involved may fire at a rate of 100 per second for several seconds and may then settle down to a relatively slow spontaneous ten discharges per second which cause no effect. Yet this slow spontaneous rate of firing keeps the pathway of response open. When a mother puts a finger in a baby's hand he sees it and feels it and his nervous system responds to this stimulus by stepping up its rate of firing beyond its spontaneous activity and a path is made in the child's nervous system perhaps for touching and grasping games (stimulus-response memory[2]).

Important learned skills, such as swimming, riding a bike, walking, eating, throwing, playing a game or an instrument, writing, drawing and painting, pronunciation and other skills, basically depend on the establishment of these patterns of nervous activity which involve mechanisms of extreme complexity at levels ranging from simple nerve pathways to the higher levels of the cortex and cerebellum. Once learned these skills are not strictly conscious and come naturally. Many are 'sensori-motor', that is based on learning by seeing as well as by doing. Most involve continuous adjustment to feedback and as such are self-adjusting.

Skills are first learned slowly and by repetition. After becoming fully established they acquire a pattern, unique to the person, the striking characteristic of which is its durability. Witness the constancy of our handwriting, a source of wonder and usefulness to our bank manager, and the long dormant skill of playing an instrument or drawing, quickly re-established after a gap of years.

The Society of Jesus for 400 years have probably spent

more time and trouble reflecting on the problems of education than any other body of people and have reached firm conclusions.

Based on their considerations and the facts about the nervous system mentioned above is my second principle: *what is well and soundly grounded in young children is likely to remain with them.* The Jesuits are well aware of this when they say, 'Give me a child until he is seven....' In the establishment of a skill it is important to associate its learning with pleasure. Enjoyment will act as a booster to learning.

Notes

1 RUSSELL, R. (1959) *Brain, Memory and Learning*, Oxford University Press
2 NORTON, A. (1981) 'Old men forget', *British Medical Journal*, 283, 6301

4 *Myelin and Early Learning*

In the last chapter I said that the nerve fibre or axon is covered by an insulating coat (myelin) and a nerve must have its myelin sheath before it can begin to conduct an impulse. The importance of this myelin can be seen in those unfortunate patients with multiple sclerosis, a condition in which the myelin begins to disintegrate. At birth the part of the brain cortex which controls physical movement (motor cortex) and a special part of the brain (the pyramidal tract) containing the nerve fibres which carry instructions from the level of the cortex to the motor nerves are not ready for action because the fibres are not myelinated. A few months after birth myelin has begun to be laid down in the tracts.

This delayed myelination is not unusual, indeed it is an essential part of a young child's survival kit. A child must learn under tuition for a long time. He must link visual information with that of other senses and relate them with bodily movements which he has initiated. He must get to know the differences between up and down, space and solid, near and far by trial and error learning so that he obtains a valid picture of the external world in which he can effectively move before he acquires myelin in his pyramidal tract. Only then does he begin to experiment in his motor behaviour. Before this the parts of the brain controlling complex instinctive behaviour keep him kicking and squirming vigorously. Between the ages of 2 and 4 when the tract has myelinated he climbs, jumps, rolls about, in short explores and enjoys using his developing motor intelligence[1].

So it is sensible to human learning that the sensory axons to the cerebral cortex carrying information from the eyes and the organs of touch, pressure, pain and so on are myelinated before the motor axons because the motor system of the brain cannot control even a simple movement unless it knows where an object is and indeed where the hand or foot is. When a toddler reaches for his toy car his eyes tell the brain where it is and the hand moves to pick it up. This apparently simple act is intricate for the brain monitors the movement of the hand ten times a second so that the approach of the hand to the toy is observed and any error corrected by the issue of fresh plans. In each of these continually reissued instructions which guide the hand to its destination the brain considers all the known implications of the movement before action. The child must not bang the toy down or it will break: 'careful', the brain warns, 'go cautiously, remember what happened before'.

The activity of the motor system then is initiated and controlled through its sensory connections; indeed the motor system is 'blind' without the information provided by its sensory input.

Myelination of the higher parts of the brain is likely to be prolonged and possibly associated with continually developing processes such as social behaviour, speech and abstract thought.

All nursery and infant teachers will know that during these early years a child revels in using his developing motor skills. It is a time when children explore tirelessly unless they are ill, with no thought of conserving energy; it is also a stage when children invent and create with ease and confidence not only in their movement but in drama, painting, in the interpretation of stories and rhymes, singing games and so on. All these activities develop gross and fine motor control but an eye needs to be kept on planning opportunities for improving both. Good use needs to be made of a school site: steps, bushes, trees, and permanent large-scale play equipment. In addition, for older children in the infant school, large and small apparatus, work with balls, moving to music, swimming, will help continue the development of their motor skills and bodily and spatial awareness. The developing motor intelligence should not be blunted by too early an introduction to specific skills and techniques or over-practising skills which at this stage impair imagination and the readiness to explore.

Notes

1 ELLIOT, H.C. (1970) *The shape of intelligence*, Allen & Unwin

5   Growth Pattern and Learning

The remarkable pattern of human growth has unfortunately been little noticed or heeded by policy makers in education. The essence of it is the early development of the brain, its protecting skull and the sense organs, particularly eyes and ears in marked contrast to the slower growth of most other parts of the body. Indeed from early foetal life the weight of the brain is nearer to its adult value than any other organ except perhaps the eye, in itself an important fact for we are primarily visual animals.

At birth the brain is 25 per cent of its adult weight whereas the whole infant body is only about 5 per cent of its adult value. At six months the brain is nearly half its adult weight. At 2½ about 75 per cent and at 5, 90 per cent with body weight about half its adult value. At 10, shortly before puberty the brain reaches about 95 per cent of its adult weight. From then on after this spurt it gains slowly whereas the body shoots up during adolescence. At about the time of puberty the brain reaches its adult pattern of brain waves.

The rapid growth of the brain and head and the relatively late development of the trunk and legs is a pattern of growth developed over the millenia which ensures that children pass through a long period when, because they are relatively small and 'weak', they can be organized and taught. To add point to this it is well known that the nervous system of animals is most sensitive to the effects of the environment during periods of fast growth, a fact which fits in with the human pattern of rapid brain growth and development of the sense organs.

During these years of swift brain growth a child's eyes, ears and touch sense in particular are absorbing experience of all kinds through imitation and exploration. It is obvious that the quality of experience is vital for sound development. In addition to sensory experience talk is as vital to human life as pure air. In this context one detail about jaw growth[1] may be added to this remarkable growth pattern. On average there is little jaw growth of any importance during the actual talking period but jaw growth is enormous in the first months of a child's life. The jaw measures about 4.5 cms a few days after birth. It is 7.5 cms at eleven months while the average for adults is about 9.5 cms. These figures provide a fascinating glimpse of speech development and emphasise the importance of speech to early learning. The brain is also programmed to match. The part of the motor cortex set aside for controlling jaw movement is four times the area of grey matter made over to controlling the trunk, a concrete illustration in the brain map already mentioned of the importance of speech (and of course feeding).

At the end of the growth spurt the child becomes an 'adult', potentially capable of reproducing, of looking after children and dominating them. Indeed at adolescence the boy becomes big and strong and, speaking in evolutionary terms adapted to such tasks as hunting, fighting and manipulating all sorts of heavy objects necessary to the food gathering activities of our ancestors and of some present-day peoples.

Some 40,000 generations of evolution have therefore made the human growth pattern useful to the survival and multiplication of the species. Throughout growth the brain is leading and dominant.

My third principle then, and one neglected by policy makers in the allocation of money, is this: *that the years from birth to puberty are a crucial time when the ability to learn is at flood readiness.* The senses are sharp, the brain is in a formative state yet general body growth is delayed. The quality of the learning environment in these formative years is vital. Of these twelve or thirteen years the pre-school and early years are of especial importance. Hand in hand with the physical spurt in brain growth, psychologists have suggested substantial intellectual growth is accomplished by aged 4[2]. The estimate is crude but serves as a rough guide to human mental development. It lends additional weight to Charles Darwin's words of a century ago when asked in which three years a man learned most. He replied, 'The first three'.

Notes

1 JESPERSON, O. (1922) *Language, Its Nature, Development & Origin*, Allen & Unwin
2 BLOOM, B.S. (1965) *Stability and Change in Human Characteristics*, Wiley

6   Crucial Times for Learning

I want to consider more specifically now brain growth in the uterus and in early life and the influences that may help or hinder its growth and development. We are all aware that bad conditions and neglect can damage physical health and kill babies and infants. It is not so obvious that they may also affect the growing brain and leave a mark on the intellect.

The brain grows very fast in the foetus. At about eight weeks from conception it weighs about 2.5 grammes while at birth it is about 380 grammes which is about 14 per cent of the total body weight. This compares strikingly with the adult brain which is about 2 per cent of body weight.

The environment of the foetus is disturbed by sounds, light and touch and it responds by moving. A century ago babies were thought to be born deaf as well as dumb, but it is known now that by mid-pregnancy the baby can hear and respond to a wide variety of sounds such as the rumbles of the intestines and the sound of the heart. In late pregnancy bright light shone at the uterus can cause movement and change in the electrical activities of the brain. Very early in pregnancy the baby responds to touch. Some parts of the brain are therefore active before birth.

The big spurt in brain growth starts towards the end of

the first six months of pregnancy and slows at around age 2. There is a smaller spurt early on from the twelfth to the eighteenth week of pregnancy. This represents the multiplication of nerve cells to their adult number and probably happens when the baby is well protected from external influences. The major growth spurt is a time when the neurones grow and develop their myelin sheaths while the dendrites branch out to form a dense network of synaptic connections. There is also then a massive multiplication of glial cells. Under a microscope a slice of grey matter from a child of six showing neurones with their sprouting dendrites looks like a dense forest of tree branches. At birth, however, there are only a few branches. As indicated earlier it is thought but not established, that the richness of branching and synaptic connections of the dendrites in the grey matter is important in the development of intelligence.

This sprouting and proliferation of the dendrites is probably under the broad guidance of heredity but the crucial point is that there is likely to be a wide margin of possibilities for development which could depend on the quality of experience provided by parents, schools and the rest of the child's environment. Educators have been quick to notice that the brain of animals provided with an enriched environment — with visual and other stimulation — results in enhanced brain weight, including an increase in the branching of the dendrites.

Judging from observations on animals, as indicated in chapter 5, the brain and nervous system are most impressionable to the effects of the environment during periods of rapid growth and development. These occur in the human brain when it is growing rapidly in the uterus and also in the years up to about 10, though it is during the first five when brain growth is especially swift.

Little is known about sensitive times in children though clear evidence has emerged that they exist in animals. A bird learns to sing and fly rapidly at an appropriate stage but progress is slow and impaired once the crucial stage is passed unexploited. It is not unreasonable to suggest that similar periods occur in children and if we could discover them education could be substantially improved by knowing what to teach and when.

Animal Experiments

To illustrate the relevance of critical times to learning I want to describe briefly some important work on brain plasticity in cats, (though similar results have been obtained in other animals) and then move on to observations on children.

If one eye of an *adult* cat is covered with an opaque substance that lets in light but not pattern, there is no change in the behaviour or electrical activity of the brain cells even after three months. Pattern can be distinguished. The cat is quite normal. Kittens on the other hand seem to be totally blind in the eye that has been covered.[1] The eye is normal but the brain is affected. Its cells do not appear to die but the nerve synapses seem to degenerate through 'lack of experience'.

We can be more precise about the timing of the critical period.[2] Other experiments with kittens show that the period of high sensitivity starts suddenly at about twenty-one days after birth, reaching peak sensitivity during the fourth, fifth and sixth weeks and declining gradually until about the fourteenth week. During the time of acute sensitivity, on the twenty-eighth day of life, only one hour of exposure to a certain pattern is enough to tune some cells in the visual area of the brain to that particular pattern.

Human Evidence

An apt example of a human sensitive period when the brain is poised to develop a particular capacity is the development of vision. Patients who have been born blind but have later regained sight are able to see only a swirling mass of colour though they may recognize objects known by touch. With time they may learn to see but it is a prolonged and difficult process quite unlike the normal acquisition of vision at the appropriate time in a child. Chapter 7 will show that the development of speech has a sensitive time when the brain is ready to develop this skill.

Caution must be exercised in extrapolating the work with cats and other animals to the growth and development of young children.[3] A child's visual environment cannot be altered in the same drastic way as in animal experiments but a few pieces of evidence exist which show that the young brain is impressionable to the effects of the visual environment. These are provided by naturally occurring eye defects — squint, cataract (present at birth or resulting from injury) and astigmatism — which mimic the unusual visual input of the cat experiments.

Broadly speaking it appears that the brain is vulnerable to the effects of abnormal vision up to the age of about 6 or 7. Damage to vision post-7 is hard to put right (squint post-3) because the visual system appears to have passed through its critical period of development. Squint for example affects vision because, if uncorrected it results in the failure of the child and future adult to develop full binocular vision with depth perception (ie to appreciate objects in 3D). Depth perception depends on the proper nerve cell connections forming to link brain cells fed by one eye with those fed by another. They have got to be in balance. By 3 they are formed and damage to vision can be irreversible if squint is not corrected before this age.

It may be noted that the period of human susceptibility is relatively much longer than in the cat since the human head as already described continues to grow rapidly over a number of years.

What might be happening to the nerve cells in the visual

cortex during the sensitive time? Probably the rapidly grow-ing neurones with their sprouting dendrites and multiplying synaptic connections have a degree of plasticity and, as in cats, become tuned to the effects of the environment. Some nerve cells may even be partially 'committed' for function allowing the environment to leave its stamp on them. For example, a nerve cell may have an inherited potentiality to develop binocularity but only does so after normal exposure to the environment. The nervous system at the level of the synapses seems no longer to be a static entity, at least in the early phase of life. Perhaps even in the adult synapses may be built up and broken down (see chapter 10).

Some facts on brain development made on the kitten's brain lend support to these speculations on the development of the human brain. Indications that the responses of a new born kitten's cortical nerve cells are partially unspecified is consistent with the fact that the number of synaptic connec-tions at birth is only 1.5 per cent of the number found in the adult. There is a dramatic rise in the number of synapses per nerve cell in the kitten's visual cortex between the seventh and thirty-sixth day of life, just the period when the kitten's brain is so sensitive to environmental modification. Micro-scopic examination of sections of the human cortex shows that the richness of nerve interconnection increases greatly over the first three or four years of life. It is quite possible that a proportion of these fast proliferating synaptic connec-tions in the kitten (and in children) are plastic and uncom-mitted. Consequently the interplay of visual experience and of inbred factors seem to create the visual cortex.

The fourth principle arising out of this work on vision simply strengthens the first by adding important detail. *Although in general we appear to pay a price for the plasticity of the young human cortex, great benefits can be bestowed through teaching because of this early adaptive plasticity. It is, however, crucial to detect visual and auditory handicaps early, at two or earlier if possible, for this allows advice and treatment to be given while the chances of improvement are high.*

Poor Food

A common anxiety is whether inefficient food in pregnancy and early life is harmful to the development of the brain. Specifically are there vulnerable times in brain development when poor food or lack of it may have serious consequences? The answer is by no means clear and to be harmful malnutrition may have to be chronic. It often happens in the economically poorer countries of the world that babies are born with light birth weights, sometimes 500 grammes below the normal weight of 2500 grammes and with small head circumference and brain weight. Such is the reserve power of the brain to catch up that, provided there are good conditions between birth and about 2, growth in head circumference in such babies is faster in the first few months after birth than in normal babies. So even chronic malnutrition in the mother may not permanently hinder catch up. The greatest risk is to children who are born below the norm of 2500 grammes and who are then malnourished. It is in these doubly deprived children where the effects on the brain are greatest.

In animal studies it is known that early malnutrition causes a reduction in the branching and growth of the brain cells, slows myelination and hampers the formation of synapses. In well-fed rats some 20,000 synapses are achieved for each single neurone in parts of the cortex. A substantial reduction is found in young starved rats with parallel alterations in behaviour and intelligence. Cell number is also reduced in various parts of the brain, myelin formation is depressed and with it nerve conduction in all the major parts of the brain.

Whether these animal experiments have any meaning

for ourselves remains an open question. It may never be answered with scientific finality because the techniques for examining the fine structure of the brain are not yet good enough. Nevertheless, even a small undetected reduction of cell number, of nerve cell growth, of myelin and synapse formation in children because of malnutrition in the uterus and in early life should be avoided in case it could harm the intellect.

Here is a telling example about IQ[4]. Korean infants who had suffered malnutrition in early infancy were examined after being adopted before the age of 3 into American homes. By 7, differences in height and weight between severely malnourished and moderately malnourished children had almost vanished. Nevertheless the Korean group as a whole remained of markedly poorer stature than American children. In contrast the IQs of the Korean children were similar to those of American children in the normal range but the originally malnourished children were less bright (by ten IQ points) than an originally well fed 'control' group of Korean children. Even so, the IQs of these malnourished children were much higher (by forty points) than the IQs of malnourished children who had returned to their own home environments.

We are witnessing here the double disadvantage spoken of a moment ago and its toll on the intellect. We may also say that the ill-effects of early malnutrition on IQ may take many years to vanish if they ever do but since malnutrition rarely occurs alone it is the sum of the disadvantages, including malnutrition which probably conspires to do the harm.

What do these results mean in everyday life here in a rich country? The evidence suggests that malnutrition reduces human achievement only when it is added to other adversity. It must be admitted to our collective shame, that it usually is but if it is compensated for sufficiently by other aspects of the environment, as well as the stimulus of tender loving care, its effects on the brain are likely to be reduced.

Nevertheless, there is a fifth broad principle to be drawn out of this complicated picture: *brain growth is bound up with body growth and so the promotion of the best general body growth possible in the period before the second or third birthday is the most that can be done to ensure good brain growth*[5].

Social and Environmental Poisons

The speed of growth of the brain *before* a child is born makes it especially sensitive to poisons during the whole of pregnancy. Indeed as well as the brain growth spurt in early childhood years, the whole nine months of pregnancy can be thought of as a sensitive period. Thus, the fast growing brain in the uterus and in the months after birth is particularly sensitive to social poisons such as alcohol, cannabis and carbon monoxide from cigarettes which move freely across the placenta. Lead from old paint, toys, food and water, as well as lead in petrol is an environmental poison. The growing brain must as far as possible be protected in the uterus from all these influences if it is to reach its true potential.

Such threats to an unborn child excite special anxiety, but if a mother slims before and during pregnancy, takes aspirin, tranquilisers or any other drug, lives by a main road with its fumes and lead dust, regularly enjoys her gin and tonic and smokes cigarettes, the risks of impaired brain growth in her baby increase. With regard to drugs, the evidence suggests that the foetus is most sensitive in the first three months of life.

The risks to the foetus of alcohol have just been mentioned. There is no doubt that heavy drinking in pregnancy can lead to poor growth, mental retardation and physical deformities in a child. The dangers to the foetus of light or moderate drinking, say one or two drinks a day, are not proven but the possibility of damage has to be kept in mind.

Individual women react to drink differently and for some women light drinking may reduce the risk to a baby but not remove it.

It is not possible to give safe upper or lower limits of drinking in pregnancy until further studies are done, but the Royal College of Psychiatrists recommend that '... women would be well advised not to drink alcohol during pregnancy ...'[6], and perhaps it would be prudent to follow this advice.

Lead Poisoning

Lead in petrol is a concern because it is being linked with impairment of a child's behaviour and intelligence. The evidence for this is not conclusive. It is likely that lead at low concentrations could never be more than a minor factor itself in pulling down IQ. Nevertheless, in combination with poor parenting, bad food and housing, even low lead levels may have their effect, like malnutrition, in impairing the brain. The removal of lead from petrol will add to the safety margin of some children who live in areas polluted by lead in plumbing, paint and industrial waste. Action to remove lead from petrol, paint and plumbing, is recommended by a Royal Commission Report[7]. Because petrol is the most clearly identifiable source of lead the report recommends that a timetable should be agreed for unleaded petrol (by 1990). The government is also asked to encourage the replacement of lead plumbing and to reduce the permissible quantities of lead in paint.

Speech

Speech will be considered in more detail in the next chapter but a child has an optimum time when his developing brain

can master the skill of talking. After about 10 a child suffer-
ing bad brain damage on the left side (the language hemisphere) may be very retarded in speech. In cases of earlier
damage, speech is lost and a period of silence follows to be
succeeded in time by a complete relearning of speech, such is
the amazing plasticity and resilience of the young brain.

Is the Brain Robust to Early Disadvantage?

All this evidence shows that the quality and nature of early
experience are crucial in animals and in young children to
the proper development of the brain's capabilities, but in
children there are likely to be periods of maximum sensitivity to learning rather than of critical times of 'now or never-
ness' as in animals. Early in life, in fact up to the brink of
puberty, it seems that some of the brain's nerve connections
are especially plastic to the influences of the environment. In
addition the whole of pregnancy is a sensitive time. These
are important facts for parents and teachers to have, particularly those concerned about the effects of early disadvantage
(as sometimes in adoption) on later achievement. Double
disadvantage for a child, that is during pregnancy and in the
early years of life, is a disastrous combination.

Nevertheless, despite early disadvantage there are hints
that if a child is normal the brain can to some extent catch
up after a bad start. Some evidence is optimistic and shows
that the 'self-righting' tendencies of the human person move
children towards normality even in the face of environmental pressures towards abnormality as the Preface suggests;
indeed, 'the possibilities for alteration in response to a
changing environment remain open for longer than has been
commonly accepted'. The Clarkes[8], whose suggestions these
are, are not concerned with the enormous importance of
heredity to later achievement (genetics and feckless parents
have much to answer for as experienced teachers know) but

solely with the effects of early environmental influences. The Clarkes' 'wedge' suggestion puts forward the notion of a greater responsiveness to the environment during early life (the thick end of the wedge) tapering off to a smaller responsiveness in adulthood and broadly fits the facts. However, the early development of the brain and sense organs well ahead of the rest of the body, a unique growth pattern developed over the millenia by evolution and the plasticity of the young human cortex, point to a sharper tailing off in responsiveness than that implied.

Much of the evidence on sensitive times is drawn from early life but the emergence of new potentialities, triggered by new stimuli, may well continue through several decades. The Court Report[8] made a telling point supportive of the crucial importance of early influences: that the disadvantages of birth and early life 'cast long shadows forward'. Nevertheless because the brain is so resilient the effects of a bad start can to some extent be diluted if love and stimulation through talk and play are given through nursery education, play group and home. But if early disadvantage is compounded in a train of poor circumstances, catch-up is less certain. My sixth principle is that *it is the compounding of poor circumstances, including those in pregnancy that conspire to harm the brain and intellect rather than the critical influence of the early childhood years in their own right.*

Notes

1 WIESEL, T.N. and HUBEL, D.H. (1963) 'Single cell responses in striate cortex of kittens deprived of vision in one eye', *Journal of Neurophysiology*, 26

2 HUBEL, D.H. and WIESEL, T.N. (1970) 'The period of susceptibility to the physiological effects of unilateral eye closure in kittens', *Journal of Physiology*, 206

3 MITCHELL, D.E. (1980) 'The influence of early visual experience on visual perception in HARRIS, C.S. (Ed) *Visual Coding and Adaptability*, Erlbaum

4 WINICK, M., *et al* (1975) 'Malnutrition and environmental enrichment by early adoption', *Science*, December

5 DOBBING, J. (1984) 'Infant nutrition and later achievement', *Nutrition Deviews*, 42, 1.

6 *Bulletin of the Royal College of Psychiatrists*, (1982) 6

7 Department of Education and Science, (1983) *Lead in the Environment*, HMSO

8 CLARKE, A.M. and CLARKE, A.D.B. (1976) *Early Experience: Myth and Evidence*, Open Books

9 Department of Education and Science, *Fit for the Future*, HMSO

7 The Gift of Speech

Like the rest of the body, the brain needs fuel, exercise of a kind and also rest. Play, exploration and conversation exercise the young brain and sleep gives it the rest it needs.

As indicated in the last chapter hearing speech is a basic human need without which a child's mind at a sensitive time of life can be starved and damaged. He may be dumb for life if he is not spoken to by the age of about 10 or at least may be very retarded in speech. It thus seems that there is an optimum time in the early years of life for the developing brain to master the skill of talking. Other aspects of language — reading and spelling — are considered in chapters 8 and 10.

Sensitive Times for Speech Development

A clue is given to the span of sensitive times by observing children who have suffered damage on the left side of the brain which from birth generally has superiority for speech and language. If the damage is sustained after about the age of 10 these children may not regain normal speech. Thankfully, permanent loss of speech is very rare though in most cases of damage IQ is lowered, perhaps because of a poorer capacity of the brain to process information. Even teenagers after a bad motor-bike accident show a remarkable capacity for recovering speech.

In cases of damage to the left hemisphere by accident or illness before the age of about 10 the brain is usually able to recover and reorganize itself and speech can be regained. Often the child's ability to convey meaning by gesture of head or hand is also lost. He is unable to nod assent in place of 'Yes' or shake his head for 'No'. It must be assumed that the characteristic gestures employed to convey meaning while speaking or instead of speaking, have nerve pathways in the speech mechanism[1].

In general the earlier the damage the less is speech impaired but the greater may be the impairment of the higher language functions — responding to nuances of meaning, completing sentences, doing anagrams for example. On the other hand, the later the damage the more likely is speech to be affected and the higher language abilities spared[2].

Though considerable plasticity and resilience of the brain are a marked feature of early life they continue in diminished form late in life. It is not surprising that the adult brain has much less plasticity to recover from accident or disease than the infant brain. Specific skills become predominantly established in one hemisphere or the other during development while the two hemispheres, as stated in chapter 2, are linked, so that balanced mental growth and functioning can take place with each hemisphere contributing to the harmonious working of the brain.

Genie

Sensitive times for learning speech are graphically illustrated by the life of Genie[3]. From the age of twenty months until her admission to hospital at 13 years 9 months Genie suffered terrible deprivation: isolated in a small closed room, tied to a potty chair where she remained nearly all the time, sometimes all night. If she made a sound she was beaten. Her father and mother never spoke to her but with her brother barked at her like dogs. Her mother was allowed to spend no more than a few minutes with her during feeding. Genie was a prisoner with no language for the crucial years between birth and puberty. Marvellously, she can now speak though only as a result of concentrated linguistic teaching for years. She is backward and as a young woman her speech is stilted, rather toneless and lacking in content. She does, however, seem to understand much more than she can say. As well as developing language, Genie can take a bus to school and has begun to express some of the basic human emotions.

It seems as if Genie had a normal brain at birth and that her left hemisphere was ready to develop language. Because she received no language stimulus the left hemisphere's development was inhibited. The meagre stimulus she obtained was through her eyes. One imagines her sitting day after day, week after week, year after year, taking in every visual stimulus, every crack in the paint, every slight change of colour and form on the walls of her prison room and looking at the pictures of old magazines that were sometimes given her to play with. The visual stimuli were sufficient for her right hemisphere to develop normally, since it, rather than the left, is more involved with understanding the environment. The left hemisphere apparently remains undeveloped.

Genie's remarkable and sad life confirms three important points. First, that the normal child learns and his brain 'strengthens', by the common experiences of childhood — talk, play, love, just like a muscle developing with exercise, Genie was deprived of these everyday experiences. Second, Genie's life also supports the general view expressed in the last chapter that normal language is more difficult to acquire after puberty. Third, it tends to confirm the strictures of the

Court Report about the harmful effect on development of a train of continuing disadvantage.

The Pattern of Speech Development

The early development of language is remarkable to follow. The evidence suggests that speech milestones are reached in a fixed sequence and at a constant age under the guidance of heredity, but there are cases, particularly in boys, where speech has started late in a child who eventually proves to be of high IQ.

What is the normal pattern of speech development?[4] Half of all children at twelve and a half months are using words with meaning and 97 per cent by twenty-one months. In the second year it is clear that children's understanding is developing rapidly but speech lags. Understanding shines in the eyes. There can be a delay of two to seven months between first hearing and utterance. Half of all children join words into simple sentences by twenty-three months and 97 per cent by three years. For both milestones girls are slightly more advanced than boys. At 3, on average, vocabulary is about 1000 words which can be put into simple sentences (subject, verb, object have appeared), and at 4 language differs from that of adults in style rather than grammar. Although girls at 5 or 6 surpass boys on average in articulation and fluency, for some measures of language development — vocabulary and verbal understanding — the boy reaches and even surpasses the girl[5]. It is the female's passion for talking and in young children the speed and extent of a girl's mastery of the mechanics of language that arouse male wonder.

Sometimes a child's expressive speech may not be too good but his understanding may be excellent. Language development is complex and the milestones given above need to be interpreted with care.

It is likely that some children who are slow to talk will often 'grow out of it' to talk normally. Nevertheless, these children may need early attention. Their difficulty may be due to one or a combination of factors including lack of appropriate stimulation, mental handicap, a hearing impairment or a specific inborn inability to acquire language normally although the acquisition of other non-language skills is unimpaired. If a child with speech delay is not helped, later difficulties at school in reading, writing and spelling are likely to compound.

Impaired hearing is a cause clearly requiring early recognition and expert treatment for reasons mentioned in the last chapter. In the other groups mentioned speech therapy, play group or nursery placement and advice and support to parents will often greatly help language development and also family morale. Of course, special classes or centres exist for a child with a disproportionately serious language handicap but many schools give positive help and encouragement — with expert advice — in normal classes. Early attention is vital but contacts between teachers in nursery classes/school and specialist services about children with special educational needs are few and need to be strengthened as do the links between teachers and parents.

Clearly from what has been said the young brain in its early stages seems to be programmed by heredity for language development but a good language environment enhances this predisposition. Even in minimally supportive environments children acquire language rapidly and mere exposure to talk even for a short period is all that appears to be necessary for a normal child to develop the competence of a native speaker. The inevitability of early language learning is strikingly shown by two Danish children brought up by their deaf mute grandmother in a remote area of Jutland. The children conversed fluently in a language no one could understand and which had no similarity to Danish[6]!

Thankfully dialect does not fully disappear even after

years away from home, for the nerve pathways for speech patterns are deeply engrained as explained in chapter 3. The native returning home soon finds that he slips back into Yorkshire or Brummy while the telephone also brings out accents not easy to pick up in ordinary speech — the flat Midland or the West Country burr.

The Mother as an Expert Teacher

There is one necessary condition for a child's poised brain to learn speech: he must have continuous and lengthy lessons from a competent speaker, his mother or father — or grandma or aunt in extended families, or someone to whom he/she can continually relate.

The mother's method of teaching language is the direct method and is the same in all lands and its methods are commonplace. The mother talks (or should talk) to the child before he can understand. From morning to night language passes over him like water from a fresh bubbling spring. Before he speaks, a good mother is on the lookout for understanding. When he says his first words she and others will egg him on. His first understanding of his mother tongue is made easier by the habits mothers have of repeating the same phrases with slight alterations and at the same time acting what they are saying:

'When I get up in the morning this is what I do; I wash my face, I brush my teeth' and so on.

Repetition is important because, as explained earlier in chapter 3, it is a basic characteristic of the brain that its nerve cells repeat patterns of activity.

Physical Changes in the Brain

But what is happening inside the brain up to the time language breaks through at about 2? And what happens between then and about 10 when the brain is losing its plasticity for speech?

All we can describe are structural changes. Nothing is known about the causes of language development which might have a physical and chemical base beyond the scope of our present tools.

What can be described is the nature of brain differences before the onset of language and after the basic skills have been acquired. Even though these observations are crude they at least tell us something about the changes in the solid stuff of the brain as it matures and thus about the physical substrate of speech.

Detailed microscopic examination shows that parts of the cortex (see diagram) controlling the power of motor (spoken) speech (Broca's area) and also the memory (association) areas mentioned in chapter 2 develop fast in the second year of life but *ahead* of these parts are those involved in the understanding of sight and sound and between these Wernicke's area concerned with understanding speech. Broca's area is within the frontal lobe just in front of that part of the motor cortex that controls speech muscles — the distorted map referred to in chapter 2. Wernicke's area occupies part of the temporal lobe and part of the parietal lobe mentioned earlier. Both Broca's and Wernicke's area are usually found in the left hemisphere.

These observations about the timing of the development of the parts of the cortex involved in speech underpin the facts of some of the speech timetable. A child understands before he can speak but at about eighteen months he can utter a recognizable word and he practises it over and over again, refining it and experimenting with the sound, egged on by an admiring audience. It is as if the brain at about 2 builds up to a springboard of development from which speech can leap forward. The nerve connections in the cortex are beginning to thicken up during the spurt in brain growth so that it looks on the very crude evidence available, as if the physical development of the brain mirrors speech development.

These facts on timing of brain development may help to explain that at about four language is well established because the underlying brain mechanisms are more or less perfected by then and act synchronously. The rapidly developing association areas represent brain tissue available for memory, a treasure house filled with the sight and sound of words. Clearly it is useful to man as a thinking, speaking animal for language to be developing and interacting in close connection with the parts of the brain concerned with memory, vision and hearing.

The Brain is Poised at Birth to Learn Speech

Besides the marvellous synchronization just spoken about, what other features of the brain make a child a specialist in learning to speak?

First, observations of the cortex by the naked eye show that it contains regions typically different in the two hemispheres[7]. The best defined is on the upper part of the temporal lobe. In the vast majority of newborn babies and adults this 'bump' is bigger on the left side and is part of Wernicke's area just mentioned. It is possible but not proven, that this speech bump represents an inborn internal machinery poised at birth to learn and understand speech and all it needs is words to set it in motion.

Confirmation that the brain is sensitive to speech at birth is shown when electrodes are placed on the scalps of infants a week to ten months old over Wernicke's area and over a corresponding area in the right hemisphere while sounds are played (words and syllables). The left hemisphere shows greater electrical activity. These striking results seem to indicate that the left hemisphere is genetically pro-grammed at birth to be sensitive to certain *structural* features of speech sounds[5].

Second, the importance of speech is reflected in the amount of motor cortex made over to it in the distorted map described in chapter 2[1].

Third, brain size is not of great importance in speech. There are dwarfs of under two feet high whose mature brain weight, though in proportion to their body, is only one-third the weight of a normal adult. Though backward they can speak as well as a 5-year-old[8]. It is not size that matters so much as the unique and profuse pattern of nerve connec-tions which cross-link areas of the brain to enable a child to connect the sight, feel and smell of a biscuit with the sound pattern of the word 'biscuit'.

Fourth, the most stunning achievement of all in speech development and one that is still shrouded in mystery, is the child's ability to scan the environment and to pick out of all the hubbub an order in language. It is known that informa-tion from the ear is relayed and re-sorted onto the auditory map in the part of the temporal lobes by the thalamus but after this a fog descends on understanding. The map must then sort out and interpret the signals as speech sounds.

I have just mentioned the wonderful sensitivity of in-fants to speech sounds. To add to that, very fine auditory discriminations can be made by babies a month old and adults across a phoneme boundary (the smallest sound units that can change meaning in a language, eg in dog /d//o//g/) so that 'd' and 't' can be distinguished[9]. In babies there is a change in pattern of sucking responses to different phonemes.

This hair breadth discrimination seems to apply to children the world over and points to some sort of inborn feature detectors in the auditory cortex suitable for processing speech. This observation is only at the foothills of understanding speech. How does the brain analyze what it hears and combine and recombine words in novel ways? After all a child learns words (for speaking, reading and writing) as they are specifically taught ('This is a door', 'this is a cat', and so on) and by listening. But then comes the next brilliant stride; he moves on to put the words he hears (or writes) into combinations never before said or heard and to make himself understood. The explanation for this remarkable feat is not in sight.

Pattern in Language

Despite our ignorance a little is known about how the brain might analyze speech. What it seems to do is to extract from it a pattern. Each spoken word will have its own pattern in time and space which is common to all the ways it can be pronounced, sung, shouted or whispered so that 'dog' will be recognized in Scotland and at the tip of Cornwall. The capacity of the brain to ignore differences in intensity, pitch and quality of the voice when identifying the sound by extracting the pattern is a wonderful gift and may well be restricted to man.

Thirty-five years ago Lord Brain[10] attempted to explain this genius of the ordinary human brain in extracting a certain pattern from a range of pronunciations. I can do no better than to quote his words:

> It is as though the meaning of the word were locked up in a cupboard which had to be opened by a key. The curious thing is that it is possible to open it by a very large number of keys which superficially seem to be very different from one another. But what makes a key open a lock is a certain kind of pattern. The pattern of the key must be appropriate to the

pattern of the lock, and if it is appropriate it does not matter whether the key is made of brass, or steel, or silver, or even gold. In the brain the patterns are very complicated electrical ones. All the possible ways of pronouncing the word 'dog' so that it can be understood have something in common; that is a certain pattern of sound. This in turn is capable of exciting in the nervous system its own particular pattern of nervous circuits, and this constitutes the key that unlocks the door which contains the meaning of the word.

It is likely that not only spoken words have an electrical pattern but that common patterns exist also in the brain for written and printed words so that no matter what the style of handwriting is or type of print, they are capable of unlocking the box containing the meaning. Visual patterns must be stored in a different part of the brain from those containing the spoken word. What seems to be important, as experienced teachers know, is to encourage children in their handwriting (and spelling) to recognize that a word is a complete piece of a pattern and that lots of words moving together rhythmically across the page make a larger pattern. Interest in pattern seems to be quite natural in any case. A young child from the start seems to be aware that to write is to make flowing, rhythmic bands of pattern. A 3 or 4-year-old watching his parent write a letter begs to write one too and scribbles his own version across a page. Good spellers seem to have the ability to see the pattern of the word 'as a whole' more easily than poor spellers. There must also be touch patterns, as the blind reading braille confirms.

Pattern will be taken further in chapter 10, for its crucial importance in many subjects — art, craft, mathematics and science — as well as in reading and spelling, is obvious.

Perhaps this weight of evidence allows my seventh

principle: *that the brain in scanning the environment, whether for sight, sound or touch, is not haphazard but searches for clues to pattern. For teaching and learning related knowledge is powerful to understanding and is remembered.*

The Language Environment

In this chapter I have concentrated on speech but the nature of the whole language environment is crucial to its development. The quality of mothering, especially early on, is as vital to the development of the brain and language as fresh air and good food is to general health because *the brain is poised at birth to learn speech.* This is my eighth principle.

The quality of mothering depends on a subtle interaction between the mother (or mother figure) and child where the mother recognizes the cues and signals in the child's babbling, clinging, grasping, crying, smiling, and responds to them. Insensitivity of a mother to a child's signals dulls that interaction and keeps it on a concrete level, because the child gets discouraged and only sends out the obvious signals for her to respond to. Only by these tiny assumptions about understanding and intelligence does the baby begin to get these qualities himself.

'Shut-down' answers and 'closed' questions harm the development of language after its natural onset. Discussion strengthens it and general mental development. By explaining, selecting or simply recounting, knowledge becomes rooted in thought and language instead of posessing but a frail hold.

Learning new words through discussion and listening will help a child to respond to demands with more precision. Once a name of an object is heard a child notices a particular element in the environment which before went unnoticed in the mass of imprecision surrounding him. Children at pre-school and the infant stage love mastering names (in a story for example) because by doing so what is named is fitted into its appropriate place or into a 'pattern'.

The homes that children come from have a 'hidden curriculum' of great importance in language development. Some parents organize their children's environment with an educational aim in mind, through books, talks and visits but their children may not have had sufficient rough and tumble play or experience of messy activities. Other children know the life of the streets and are not short of group play and language experience. They run errands, have their gangs and street games, help dad to build a pigeon loft and go to football matches and whippet races but they may not get the massive back-up from home of books, of explanations and opportunities to learn new words. Some may never have had the experience of looking at the pictures of a story book as its text is read to them. Many of the homes these children come from are certainly not uncaring. Other children live in rural poverty but may know a good deal about trees and wild life, soil, rocks, farm implements, machinery, birth and death.

The impact of the experiences children bring with them to school is determined by the words they know. If they are lacking, the value of the experiences is blunted unless the words are supplied.

Schools therefore need to capitalize on individual experiences but also compensate for deficiencies and adjust to the individual child's needs with appropriate experiences. Children who live in rowdy public conditions need more quiet areas to learn to read quietly, to paint, listen to stories and look at the pictures and ask questions to clear up misunderstandings about language or illustrations. Children from urban back streets need to experience more living and growing things in schools and to talk and write about them and paint them. Children who live in isolated farms and in hamlets need to experience cooperative activity in art and science which brings with it language and social interaction. Individual needs are stressed because generalization is sterile in this context.

Finally, sometimes silence is the best help and too much well-meant interference with explanations and books can destroy the silent sensory pleasures of looking, feeling, smelling and listening.

Notes

1 PENFIELD, W. and ROBERTS, L. (1959) *Speech and Brain Mechanisms*, Princeton
2 DICKENSON, J.W.T. and McGURK, H. (1982) *Brain and Behavioural Development*, Surrey University Press
3 FROMKIN, V. *et al* (1974) *Brain and Language*, 1
4 ROBINSON, R.J. (1982) 'The child who is slow to talk' *British Medical Journal*, 285
5 HARRIS, J.H. (1977) 'Sex Differences in the growth and use of language' in DONALDSON, E. and GULLAHORN, J. (Eds) *Women: A Psychological Perspective*, Wiley
6 JESPEDSON, D. (1922) *Language, Its Nature, Development and Origin*, Allen & Unwin
7 GALABURDA, A.M. *et al* 'Right left asymmetries in the brain' *Science*, 199
8 MILLER, G.A. (1972) 'Linguistic communication as a biological process' in PRINGLE, T.W.S. (Ed) *Biology and the Human Sciences*, Oxford University Press
9 SUTHERLAND, N.S. (1973) 'Object recognition', *Handbook of Perception*, 3, Academic Press
10 LORD BRAIN (1950) 'Speech and thought' in LASLETT, P. (Ed) *The Physical Basis of Mind*, Blackwell

8　*Double Brain*

A century ago whole regions of the cortex were being studied to find out whether different parts had the same or different functions. Now minute areas and tiny groups of cells are being investigated to discover whether there is a basic function common to all areas of the brain. Work is advancing rapidly and it is likely that some of the elusive secrets of the hemispheres will be revealed in the next generation. The range of facts available is large but a synthesis of them by some Darwin of the mind is the master stroke necessary. Education will benefit because a sound theory of brain function will be available to help us understand better how we read, how to teach children to read and spell with, for us, greater understanding of their difficulties, how we see shapes, how patterns of sound, sight and touch are analyzed and so on.

Chapter 2 described the hemispheres in some detail but a brief reminder may be helpful. The two hemispheres have superiorities for different mental processes. In most right-handed people the left hemisphere is specialized for language, logic and numbers and seems to process information analytically and sequentially feature by feature. The right has superiority for visuo-spatial functions — the appreciation of whole integrated images for example. The hemispheres are linked by a tough nerve strap so that information can be shared and a unity of thought and behaviour achieved.

Tucked inside each of the temporal lobes (chapter 2) is the hippocampus. Experiments with animals[1] and earlier observations by the brain surgeon Wilder Penfield suggest that the cells in the left hippocampus may perhaps be a mapping system for the placing of words. As already explained, a child understands what is said to him and utters combinations of words never before said or heard and is understood without the child or the listener being aware of the novelty. All of this remarkable activity may be mediated by electrical and chemical signals in cells in the mapping system of the left hippocampus.

Our right hippocampus may perhaps be a spatial mapping system inherited from our animal ancestors. In animals such as the rat the hippocampus seems to act as a map which captures in its cells the spatial layout of an animal's experienced environment. The map can be used in finding food and water, mates, safe havens and so on. These cells in the hippocampus signal (by an electrical discharge) an animal's position in its environment by summing up the stimulus from several spatial clues, about the position of water for example[1]. A cell may signal rapidly when an animal faces in a particular direction and slow down when it is not. Another may fire rapidly on rounding a corner.

We must be careful in extending animal experiments to ourselves but the maps for language and for our spatial environment are quite possibly in the left and right hippocampus. Of significance for education both the maps will be dynamic and susceptible for learning. A greater knowledge of the work of the left in conjunction with the adjacent temporal lobe will possibly give us more understanding of language development including reading, while a knowledge of the working of the right in association with its temporal lobe will give us more understanding about the way children learn about those subjects which require spatial abilities.

Several investigations have suggested earlier and greater activity in the right hemisphere probably enhanced by a better blood supply.[2] This is not surprising because for most of our evolution we were predominantly spatial creatures and our problem-solving and thinking were based on right hemisphere activity. Chapter 4 pointed out that a child needs to obtain early in life a plan of his world in which he can safely move. The potential for developing spatial skills is perhaps genetically programmed to be well advanced in young children. In support of this suggestion general brain damage in the first year of life favours the sparing of spatial rather than verbal skills[3], perhaps because they are of more 'basic' importance (finding direction for example) or because they are more diffusely represented throughout the brain.

Boys and Girls: Chromosome Differences

What pointers arising out of a knowledge of the work of the hemispheres are there for teaching and learning? At least three: the controversial topic of mental differences between boys and girls; reading; and the need for breadth and balance in the curriculum.

To understand the roots of sex differences we must look briefly at heredity and the chromosomes. This is taken further in chapter 11. The chromosome outfit of men and women differs slightly. Each has twenty-three pairs of chromosomes in each cell of the body, one pair determining sex. In men this pair consists of a large X and a small Y chromosome. In women there are two X chromosomes and it is the absence of a Y that makes for femaleness. The other twenty-two pairs of chromosomes, the non-sex chromosomes, are called the autosomes. The development of the

embryo in the absence of a Y chromosome is then, relent-
lessly to a female pattern. It is the Y chromosome that carves
maleness from a basically female mould. Eve, so the Old
Testament says, was carved from a rib of Adam but it is
rather the reverse.

During reproduction the twenty-three pairs of chromosomes divide to form gametes each carrying one chromosome of each pair — twenty-three chromosomes. In the
male; therefore, there are two kinds of sperm, a Y-carrier
and an X-carrier. The female eggs are all the same, all carry
an X chromosome. A Y-carrying sperm fusing with an egg
creates a male embryo (XY) and restores the double number
of chromosomes. An X-carrying sperm fusing with an egg
produces a female embryo (XX). So in essence the sex differences depend on a simple switch: the presence of a Y
chromosome possessed by men but absent in women. The
XY combination triggers the development of testes, the XX
combination ovaries.

In newborn rats the testes produce the male hormone
which acts as a chemical signal travelling in the blood to sex
a key part of the brain, the hypothalamus, one of whose
functions as explained in chapter 2 is to regulate the repro-
ductive cycle. In the absence of a Y and the consequent
absence of male hormone, female development goes on. In
ourselves the Y chromosome must deliver its signal to the
brain and hypothalamus long before birth to set in train the
development of the sex organs. There is no hard evidence,
however, that the sexing of the human hypothalamus or
other parts of the brain depends upon the male sex hormone
as in the rat. We can only speculate that it acts in a similar
manner.

Sometimes mistakes are made during reproduction
when the chromosome pairs divide and when a sex chromosome may be lost from a gamete or added to it. When a Y is
lost fusion of the abnormal sperm with a normal egg produces an XO embryo instead of XY with forty-five chromo-

somes instead of forty-six. If this unfortunate error is not screened out by natural abortion during pregnancy it gives rise to a sterile female with no general mental defect but possessing what is probably a specific error in the parietal region of the cortex[4] (chapter 2) to cause 'space-form' blindness. In some instances this is so bad that the carriers of the chromosome error cannot find their way about using simple road maps and also do badly in tests involving shape and pattern. This example underscores the fact that each chromosome carries its own unique pedigree on its back which can profoundly influence the development of the brain but their effects are only seen in gross chromosome mistakes. The most common (though not an error of the sex chromosomes but involving an extra and particular autosome to give forty-seven chromosomes) gives rise to Downs syndrome (mongolism) and the effect on the brain, intellect and personality is profound.

Behavioural Plasticity in the Sexes

While there are subtle anatomical differences between the hypothalamus of males and females perhaps triggered by the male hormone and which cause the hypothalamus to stimulate the pituitary gland beneath it to release the appropriate sex hormones, elsewhere in the brain anatomical differences have not been found. In any case it is likely that critical differences will be in fine anatomical structure rather than in gross measures such as shape and area.

In support of the notion of a 'common brain structure' in males and females it is clear that most, or all, of the animals in a species appear to have the brain 'circuitry' for the behaviour of both sexes. For example, electrical stimulation of the hypothalamus of male rats elicits 'female' behaviour such as pup-carrying and nest building as well as male behaviours. If female rats are removed from a colony the males take over the care of the young. It seems on this evidence that the circuitry for a wide repertoire of behaviour for both male and female is laid down genetically and that the hormones and environment select one set or the other.

A similar illustration of plasticity lies in predatory behaviour in the cat[5]. Whether or not an adult cat kills, hates, fears or plays with rats is strongly determined by rearing. Most cats reared with mothers who killed rats ended up as rat killers themselves. When kittens were reared in isolation slightly less than half of them killed rats. Yet it has been shown that electrical stimulation of the appropriate areas of the brain of non-killing kittens elicits the full sequence of rat killing behaviour. It appears that although the genes programme the behaviour, the environment, which includes upbringing determines whether it will ever be used.

Turning to ourselves, gender identity seems to depend largely on whether a child is reared as a girl or a boy even when this is in contrast to its biological sex. Once gender identity has been established it cannot be reversed easily and by five it is usually firmly entrenched.

There is a parallel between the process of gender identity formation and the acquisition of speech. By four or five most children have a good grasp of the main linguistic principles of their native tongue. At the same time identification with one sex or the other is a firm part of the child's self-image.

All this evidence seems to underline the extraordinary degree of behavioural plasticity in ourselves. It shows that one of our most important behavioural patterns (gender) is developed early by social interaction and imitation. It allows a ninth principle: *man has developed a great capacity for imitation and the most powerful of all didactic tools is the exemplar of parents and teachers.*

Mathematics and Science

While there is strong evidence in ourselves for a considerable degree of behavioural plasticity it is not total and differences must be underpinned by the effect of the sex chromosomes on the brain.

On *average* all the language functions mediated by the left hemisphere are slightly ahead by about two months in girls of 4 and 5 compared with boys of the same age. Then, and probably for much longer, linguistic skills play a larger part in the thinking and problem solving of girls. In boys non-verbal spatial functions mediated by the right hemisphere are more developed and boys' capacity for spatial work with patterns and shapes and in particular for rotating them mentally into new positions, is better, even from the age of 2. Most important, boys excel in the exploration of things, crucial in science and the learning of mathematics. In the early stages mathematics and science are not learned through talk but by experimenting under skilled guidance.

Much of the material and equipment used in play and more formal work contributes to the development of simple scientific and mathematical ideas. Woodwork, waste materials and play with blocks, will promote awareness of shape, size and the relationship of one piece to another; use of balances and scales helps to develop concepts of 'heavy' and 'light' while everyday observations — the hands of a clock turning through angles, calendars — promote mathematical ideas. Given time boys will catch up on language but girls may not catch up so easily on practical experiences that involve mathematical and scientific ideas.

In the preceding few paragraphs I have made use of some average differences between boys and girls but there is a devastating tendency among some to think that average values tell all that needs to be known. Sexuality lies on a continuum and all men have some degree of femininity and all women possess some degree of masculinity. Certainly many girls far surpass many boys in mathematical and scientific ability and those that do would benefit from less discouragement than they commonly encounter.

Whatever factors cause the differences in mathematical ability in boys and girls, biological and/or environmental, they appear to be in operation by the time children are in the primary school as indicated in the DES Assessment of Performance Unit report of 1982[6]. So just as early practical experience is crucial for progress in science, early experience of number relationships by *doing* may be especially important for girls.

While upbringing and tradition are important and the plasticity of our behaviour a well established fact, inherited factors largely based on the sex chromosome switch cannot be ignored. Thus my tenth principle is *that more numerical, experimental and spatial activities should be stage-managed for girls so that they will learn through manipulation and experiment as well as through talk.*

Reading

We can only speculate about reading and brain function because evidence is sparse about the acquisition of reading skills but speech and listening are an essential foundation to it. The inherent quality of the brain to search for patterns must be important as well so that, for instance, similarities and differences in sounds and in shapes of letters are noticed. The first and most important contribution of home and school to literacy, however, is to develop a child's command of spoken language.

The two hemispheres, as I have indicated, function as an integrated system so that when a child reads his right hemisphere perhaps assists in recognizing the position and sequence of words while the clues to meaning given by individual words are interpreted by the left hemisphere. When position and meaning are integrated by both halves of the brain working together the passage is understood.

When a young child stumbles on a difficult work in his book he is likely to stick on that word rather than let his eyes rove a little way ahead to try to gain clues to meaning from the rest of the passage unless the teacher points to pictures and discusses possibilities in the story. Although young children certainly are helped to read by having a variety of methods available to them, reading now by the look of the word, now by its initial sound, now by guessing meaning from context clues, reading essentially involves looking for meaning and not decoding specific words. It is interesting in this regard that the eyes are a second or so ahead of the voice as if the brain attempts to understand the print by keeping slightly ahead of the flow of detail that it is trying to handle[7]. If the child's eyes move from the words to scan ahead as they do naturally, he might lose his place and spatial activity in recovering it might possibly jam the work of the left hemisphere which is trying to integrate the clues to meaning. The old method of marking the difficult word by putting a finger on it and letting the eyes rove for meaning clues allows the eyes to come back to the finger without effort. Finger, brain and eye work closely together and the brain is not troubled in finding its place. The finger acts as a solid point of reference so that the brain, using the eyes to scout ahead, can make decisions about meaning and thus about individual words in advance. In a way the brain is acting like a walker who is lost and pauses by some known spot marked on his map, and decides from a look at the ground ahead which way to go. He is thinking about and integrating clues but his position is firm.

When a good reader tackles a difficult book he may unconsciously break down difficult passages into manageable sections mainly by right hemisphere activity. In doing so the speed of reading slows up: brain, eye and voice converge on the same point and the natural scanning ahead for meaning clues disappears[7]. The pauses in between the chunks help him to think about the author's meaning by using his left hemisphere. In a familiar text the eyes scan ahead. A child over-concentrating on individual words tends to miss the overall meaning of the passage perhaps because overactivity on one side of the brain blocks activity on the other.

Four and 5-year-olds are sometimes introduced too quickly to reading schemes and phonic methods and spend much time decoding print so that they read mechanically and without much interest in, or understanding of, the content. The result is lack of progress and confusion. At a certain stage a child can make progress by practising recognition and pronunciation of individual words without attempting to grasp the general sense of a passage. But if he is not simply going to 'bark at the print', soon he must be led to understand that the phrase and then the sentence and even the passage are in reality the units which communicate the story which the author sets out to tell.

Parents and teachers of young children can demonstrate this by reading the story aloud with the child sitting beside them watching. Clearly, some children grasp the need to scan ahead to establish an understanding more readily than others. It is, however, an essential step for every child. The HMI report on primary education[8] emphasized this and said that when the child becomes more proficient and once the skills of decoding are established further skills should be introduced including skimming and scanning passages to establish the main points and the interpretation of context clues. When doing this it seems likely that the two halves of the brain collaborate as the child reads and understands the passage.

These speculations about brain function and reading are, of course, crude and make the brain sound like a clumsy two-way machine rather than something that resembles a complexity of modular computers.

To help in the early stages of reading children need books which are attractive and relevant to their interests, experience and imagination and also to see their teachers turning to books with enjoyment. If the material is dull with no relevance to any prior knowledge they may have, reading will become more difficult and they will cease to scan naturally for context clues and stick on bits of the text. Many infant teachers have had marked success in teaching reading by typing out children's own stories on a jumbo typewriter and using them as reading material. Unfortunately children's reading of stories is not always part of the planned daily programme of schools and it is seen as something to be enjoyed once the set tasks are finished.

Teachers of older primary age children will recognize not only poor reading skills in children who are generally backward, emotionally deprived and culturally disadvantaged, but also the specific problem. Impaired reading (especially in boys) despite at least average skills in art, craft and playing an instrument is one. Some of these specific developmental problems, including dyslexia (a selective reading disorder) or visuo-spatial disturbances, are frequently of constitutional origin and may have their roots in maturational failures in precise regions of the brain. Quite often with dyslexia, indeed in almost 90 per cent of cases, there is a family history of speech defect and/or reading and spelling difficulties[9]. A specific remedial programme based on early analysis of the individual child's difficulties is essential to prevent a progressive deterioration in morale and self-esteem even at the infant stage. One key feature in the success of any programme is the need to reassure yet still present the child with real demands.

Balance in Learning

Just as the body needs a balanced diet to grow and keep healthy, so knowledge of the brain confirms that a child

needs a balance of experience to develop the full potential of both hemispheres. Genie's left hemisphere was undeveloped by hearing no language.

The work of nursery and primary schools is not compartmentalized and the experiences offered to the children foster this balance. In the nursery school/class, learning language and number skills is most effectively achieved through play, exploration and practical activities. The framework of planning in the best infant schools gives priority to reading, writing and mathematics but these basic skills are strengthened through a broad programme of work which includes music, art and craft and work on the physical and natural environment. Most of these activities involve both sides of the brain collaborating quite naturally. Drawing, model-making and painting have a bias to right hemisphere activity. Mathematics inclines to the left but geometry must involve the right. Reading uses both, as does science. Experiment and analysis is mainly left hemisphere activity, but understanding shape is mainly right-sided. Writing and spelling involve pattern and spacing (right hemisphere) and meaning (left).

As children grow older and specialization increases the strength of the right hemisphere can be neglected. There is a discipline in dance, sculpture, painting, drawing, drama and music different but equally as rigorous and precise as that in mathematics and science and these 'performance' subjects are essential to balanced development. The HMI report on primary education commented on the deterioration in standards of two and three-dimensional art and craft work from age 7 while drawing or modelling from direct observation was rarely encouraged. Much later on academic pupils in the secondary school also may suffer from the loss of aesthetic and creative subjects[10] and the capacity to respond emotionally and intellectually to sensory experience may be hampered.

Alfred Whitehead[11] put his finger on the need for

balance when he wrote, '. . . in teaching you will c͏
grief as soon as you forget that your pupils have b
. . . .', adding, '. . . It is a moot point whether the hur
hand created the human brain or the brain created the han͏
. . .' In this respect the hand/speech connection is strong in
the brain. The parts of the grey matter that control speech
and hand movement — the tongue, jaw and lips and the
thumb and fingers — are close together. This is practically
illustrated when a needle is threaded or a child concentrates
hard in drawing or writing when the tongue often pokes
out! Thus hand skills need to be developed from an early age
because it is likely that they will make a big contribution to
the development of the language 'territory' of the brain — a
special relationship recognized by Maria Montessori[12]:
'Man, we may say, takes possession of his environment by
his hand, and transforms it as his mind directs'. Hard evidence for the hand skill/language link is not yet crystal clear
but it is known that a girl who excels in drawing and
painting is also likely to have excellent verbal skills. The
connection for some reason seems weaker in boys[13].

Commonsense and experience suggests that neither side
of the brain should be neglected in education. Children
need a broad experience which develops the potentialities of
both hemispheres. A mind that understands only words and
numbers is parched and may come to lack sensitivity and to
lose touch with the solid reality of everyday things and with
the feelings of other people.

It must be admitted that precise knowledge of brain
anatomy and function contributes little to what I have just
discussed. Most derives from experience and observations of
children's behaviour and what the brain is actually doing can
only be cautiously deduced. *It is prudent, however, to plan
to make full use of the strengths of both hemispheres. By
exercising the rather under-used right hemisphere the performance of both might be improved.* This is the eleventh
principle.

Notes

1 O'KEEFE, T. and NADEL, L. (1979) 'The hippocampus as a cognitive map', *The Behavioural & Brain Sciences*, 2

2 HARRIS, L.J. (1975) 'Neuropsychological factors in the development of spatial skills' in *Children's Spatial Development*, Charles Thomas

3 DICKENSON, J.W.T. and McGURK, H. (1982) *Brain and Behavioural Development*. Surrey University Press

4 DARLINGTON, C.D. (1978) *The Little Universe of Man*, Allen & Unwin

5 KUO, Z.Y. (1931) 'The genesis of the cat's responses to the rat', *Journal of Comp Psychol*, 11

6 *Assessment of Performance Unit: Summary Report No 11*, DES (1982)

7 SMITH, F. (1978) *Understanding Reading*, Holt

8 Department of Education and Science, (1978) *Primary Education in England*, HMSO

9 MORRIS, J. and SPINKS, T. (1986) 'Specific difficulties', *Times Educational Supplement*, 21 February

10 Department of Education and Science (1979) *Aspects of Secondary Education*, HMSO

11 WHITEHEAD, A. (1932) *The Aims of Education*, Williams & Norgate

12 MONTESSORI, M. (1936) *The Secret of Childhood*, Longmans

13 HARRIS, J.H. (1977) 'Sex differences in the growth and use of language', in *Women: a psychological perspective*, Donaldson, E. and Gullahorn, J. (Eds.), Wiley

9 Learning by Playing and Exploration

When a child starts infant school at 5 some parents are inclined to grumble because they think that their child is playing about too much and not working. When a job is easy we say it's 'child's play'. Frowning on child's play has a long history perhaps stemming from the Protestant work ethic. John Wesley warned that, 'He who plays as a boy will play as a man' but exploration and play possibly help a child's brain to develop by improving his language and intellect, by extending his physical skills and by preparing the ground for the initiation of emotional relationships. The experiences gained through play must be stored in the brain cells as part of a child's 'model of the world', an idea elaborated in chapter 10. The brain's model developed through experience will help a person to make predictions and also decisions about the situations likely to be encountered.

Play

Play has deep roots, not only in ourselves but in most other animals but what play is for is not entirely clear. One suggestion is that it helps to train for independent adult life, but in many animal species there is no evidence that an animal that has not played is unsuccessful as an adult.

Most of the learning is left to the young themselves, so that a mother cat will take a live incapacitated mouse to her kittens, but it is left to them to use the mouse to practise on. In rats play has a critical time in which it must develop. Social play starts at about seventeen days old but dies away and stops when the rats are about seven weeks old. If young rats are isolated during this time they show severe learning difficulties as adults. It is not possible to generalize. Mice which do not play when young suffer no impairment in adult behaviour if they are isolated. It is well known that depriving young rhesus monkeys of play with others during their first year of life hampers them from having proper social and sexual relationships as adults, though this could be due to a range of problems — perception and learning impairment — not merely absence of play.

Our own particular forms of play are unique and depend upon our large brain which has its instructions for behaviour sketched in lightly by heredity. Corinne Hutt[1] divided children's play up into broadly three groups: games with rules, exploratory play and imaginative play. All these forms of play in the under-fives can intermix as a child 'plays'. Games with rules like hopscotch, marbles, street football or 'tag' have strict rules but children under 5 have only very hazy ideas about rules and are even hazier about the need to stick to rules. Games in the adult sense, when to put it in rather grandiose terms, children can learn the essence of morality by 'playing the game', only really begin in adolescence.

Exploratory play is complex and includes a spectrum of problem-solving activities such as a 2-year-old doing puzzles and jigsaws. It can be productive when a child of 4 makes a ship out of boxes and other materials so that he works towards a definite end product. It can also be truly exploratory in the sense of finding out by inspection and investigation so that a child asks as he approaches a toy, 'What does this object do?'

Play can also be imaginative and involve an element of fantasy as when a 4-year-old becomes a doctor and acts the part or sits on a box that becomes a fire engine or becomes 'mother' or 'father' in domestic play.

Most children of about 5, however, distinguish between 'work' and play. When a 5-year-old (and of course an older infant child) is being a space ship he knows very well that it is imaginative play and will move out of such play with ease. He will, for example, stop to ask a direct question of a companion on quite a different subject ('Did you like the sausages?') and then move back into play again.

Play and Exploration

Imaginative play is rather different from exploration and usually has an element of fun in it. It has freedom and is satisfying for its own sake. Exploration is usually serious, concentrated activity and involves investigation and manipulation and a desire to succeed. Sometimes play follows exploration, so that a 5-year-old seriously explores how to use his tricycle. Once he has got the feel of it he may 'play' at cornering fast and ride rapidly back and forth. In other words, he has fun with his tricycle. He plays! That is, he applies for his own amusement what he has previously learned through exploration. An older child will do the same when bouncing a ball, spinning a top, skipping and so on. When these physical skills are being acquired children are involved in concentrated activity. Only after they have mastered them do they have fun and play!

Underlying these observations of behaviour, striking differences in body function can be measured in children playing and exploring which strengthen the idea that the two activities have different roles. When a child is exploring the blood flow to certain parts of the brain increases. Besides this differential blood flow it has been noticed by the Hutts[2] that when a child is relaxed heart beats are not exactly regular and when he is concentrating this choppiness is suppressed. In imaginative play the heart rate is most variable and least during problem solving. Exploration shows an intermediate position. All these physical indicators show that the brain and nervous system work at a higher pitch during the non-play activities.

What might this mean in terms of learning? One view is that imaginative play contributes little to intellectual growth, which I shall say more about in a moment, but exploratory learning, if the ingredients are present — security, a minimal amount of interference from adults, intervention and extension at the right time, time and an environment which invites exploration and in which it can progress — may be the more productive.

Three details, which apply to all forms of play, may be added: on intervention, time and environment. Successful intervention is of crucial importance if play activities are to be developed to the full. Too often once equipment and materials are provided teachers remain aloof from play or engage in other activities such as hearing children read while play is taking place. On intervention, Christian Schiller[3] once wrote aptly: 'The headmaster of the best junior school I have ever known said this, "I always say to teachers, leave the children alone until they need help: but remember that they probably won't come and tell you when that moment comes. To seize that moment is the art of teaching young children"'. Many children, for example, have access to model railways, layout of local streets and shops, toy farms and so on which are used for play but because of failure to intervene at the right moment, spatial concepts are neglected, especially the idea of scale.

Christian Schiller's headmaster was right about the art of seizing the right moment to intervene in play. Intervention too soon may impede learning, for a child must be allowed to do things over and over again. This is because he must reassure himself that what he has learned is true about weight, texture, softness, hardness and countless other things; in general, that certain patterns repeat themselves.

With regard to time, children should not be bustled from one activity to another otherwise they will become hasty and unabsorbed. To provide time does not mean leaving children in a vacuum; intervention and an environment conducive to exploration are necessary ingredients but concentration and a desire to succeed are important aspects and values of play. A child's concentration span is longer than a teacher may demand for a task and the child sets his own limits. He can 'fail' anything within these limits and accept it without damaging his self-esteem and self-image both of which can be enhanced by play.

The environment of many nursery and infant classes inspires experiment, imagination and talk. A few hamper these attributes and activities by a too orderly classroom leaving no room for adventure, physical or mental.

Participation Learning

The exploratory drive starts soon after birth. A baby will start to explore his mother, himself and his surroundings with his eyes and will gradually learn to move his toes and fingers and to reach out for objects. When he can crawl he is soon exploring everything. By these means he is getting to know about the properties of things.

Continual and active exploration are essential to acquire and retain good motor visual coordination. Experiments with kittens prevented from seeing their forelimbs by a high collar showed that they could not reach or strike accurately because of a failure to integrate limb movement with visual information[4].

A more elegant demonstration of the importance of exploratory activity in visual learning is again seen in littermate kittens who spent several hours a day in a contrivance which allowed one kitten some freedom to explore, just like a normal kitten, while the other was suspended passively in a gondola[5]. By a simple mechanical arrangement this was moved in all directions by the exploring litter mate so that the gondola passenger was subjected to the same play and visual imagery as the active kitten; but, of crucial importance, none of this activity was initiated by the passenger. His visual world was passively provided for him just as it is for us on a TV screen (a good point for us in its own right). When not in this contraption both kittens were kept with their mother in darkness. After some weeks, tests show that the active kitten had learnt to use its visual fields for providing a valid 'representation' of the external world in the brain which could be used for the purpose of movement just as well as a normal kitten, whereas the gondola passenger had learnt nothing.

One simple example of this difference was shown by placing the kittens on a narrow shelf which they could leave either on one side with a small drop or on the other side with an intimidating drop. (Actually a transparent shelf prevented any untoward damage in falling off on the 'dangerous' side.) The actively trained kitten always picked the easy side; the passive chose either in random manner.

The important conclusion from these and many other observations and experiments on animals and man, and one which supports the thesis of chapter 4, is that exploration is essential if we are to build up in the brain a representation or 'model', sensed by sight, touch and movement, which is useful for the accurate interpretation of the world. This model is further discussed in the next chapter. The twelfth principle that arises from this is *that a child does not learn from a passive kaleidoscope of experiences but from the outcomes of actions that he or she has initiated.*

Man is no different from many other animals in his need for trial and error learning in order to be able to interpret visual and other cues accurately. A striking example of exploratory behaviour and of learning through it in a one year old is given by the ethologist, Niko Tinbergen[6].

> A twelve month old boy guarded by his aunt and grandmother was observed crawling about over a sandy slope which was bare but for isolated rosettes of ragwort and occasional thistle plants. After having moved over ragwort rosettes without showing any reaction to them, he happened to crawl over a thistle whose prickly leaves slightly scratched his feet. Giving a barely perceptible start, he crawled on at first but stopped a second or so later and looked back over his shoulder. Then, moving slightly back, he moved his foot once more over the thistle. Next he turned to the plant, looked at it with intense concentration, and moved his hand back and forth over it. This was followed by a perfect control experiment: he looked round, selected a ragwort rosette and touched it in the same way. After this he touched the thistle once more and only then did he continue his journey ...

The exploring child was behaving very much like a scientist, that is he was learning about the nature of things by direct observation and experiment. A child cannot be taught in words because he will not understand. He experiences the world he meets by touching, looking, listening and smelling. He draws his conclusions, then he tests them, just like the 1-year-old returning to touch the thistle and the ragwort.

The Importance of Sensory Experience

This way of building up knowledge of the world through our senses and by trial and error is the basis of all later intellectual activity. Few of us have developed all our senses as fully as we might. Judging distance, rate of movement, distinguishing colours, shapes and sizes, are learned by experience sometimes after a child reaches school age. For practical purposes it is important to give children maximum sensory experience by having plenty of things around them to explore.

Children have much visual experience but perhaps not enough experience of touch and it is good to see young children at nursery school making up for this by experimenting with the touch sense. Sight and touch are two senses which are of paramount importance in helping us to interpret the world. We have inherited an eye that by day is as sharp as a needle so that detail can be detected ten times finer than a cat can resolve. We are also quite good at seeing in the dark. Owls are only two-and-a-half times as sensitive to light as we are[7]. Our colour and depth vision are good. But of the two, touch is the 'reality' sense[8] as a bumped head bears witness. It has a solidity that vision alone cannot give. Touch provides two or three independent checks about an object — movement, temperature, texture. It may also be heard. Sight and touch together are powerful yet precise tools for providing us with correlative information. All the senses acting together provide check and double-check.

An important related aspect of touch is that people are marvellously adapted for active rather than passive touch because we can learn more about the world by having the nervous system so adapted. If, for example, shapes are pressed into the palm of the hand (passive touch) they are less accurately identified than if they are accessible to exploration by the finger tips (active touch). A child's exploring fingers are an extension of his eyes or vice versa.

I mentioned in chapter 2 that certain parts of the cortex are devoted to each of the senses. For touch there is about twenty times more space of the grey matter devoted to the face, especially the lips, and to thumbs and fingers than to the trunk. In the pig, the touch area, linked to the snout, is as big as the visual cortex. Our fingers and lips are as important to us for exploration as its snout is to the pig.

What Use is Imaginative Play?

From what I said a moment ago there is clearly a fundamental difference between imaginative and exploratory play. One rather extreme view is that imaginative play contributes little to intellectual growth. It may however act as a yeast to children's imagination. It has also been speculated that such play may be necessary to keep the infant brain primed and active. Even when they are doing nothing adults and older children have their thoughts to keep the brain active. A young child has to develop this internal thinking and until it develops, which it does gradually through the primary school years, play in all its forms acts to keep the brain pepped up. So play could help children to move towards the ability to think without external stimulation; children under 5 can only really think by doing, looking, listening, touching and so on.

Corinne Hutt[1], writing about imaginative play, echoes the uncertainty and suggests that no one seems to be clear where its merits lie. There is among teachers, however, the strong feeling that a child who engages in imaginative play is 'creative' and that this assists other areas of intellectual activity. There is no evidence as yet that such creativity is related to superior performance in any other intellectual skill. For example, it does not seem to assist in encoding in the memory an experience (a visit to the fire station or farm) significantly more deeply than by simply talking about the visit afterwards or painting it. Experiments on learning about conservation skills (to decide whether or not two equal balls of clay contained the same amount after one had been deformed) which included an element of imaginative play had no effect on conservation judgments made by pre-school children[9].

Imaginative play, nevertheless, is a strong part of human make-up. It must, as exploratory activity does, have an inherited base and have been selected for in evolution and therefore be of use to our species. What might this use be?

Sometimes a new (painful) experience for a child cannot be accepted until the child has acted it out over and over again in imaginative play and the particular experience is thus brought into perspective and control. A sudden visit to a hospital is a shock and he may play at doctors and nurses for weeks. Children playing at dentists and patients prior to a visit not only increase their knowledge and powers of observation but such play may help to allay fears so that they can accept and understand similar situations. We all rehearse for things that might happen to help us face them if they do, but adults rehearse in their minds, children in their play; doing so is remedial and has survival value.

Imaginative play has another key role in human biology: it helps a child who imitates someone — a parent, teacher, milkman — to find out what it feels like to be that person which is a step towards being able to cooperate which is a basic human requirement ('men and women have tendencies to love and help much more than hate each other'[10]) obscurely related to the functions of the frontal lobes (chapter 2). To cooperate requires an understanding of behaviour and by pretending a child learns something about this. Perhaps in this way imaginative play may gradually help a child to learn how to cope better with conflict situations because he will then begin to understand in a small way what it is like to be in someone else's shoes.

Of crucial importance, a child is helped to think symbolically by imaginative play. In this he sometimes treats an object as something else which is not present, that is as a symbol. The power of symbolism is a unique human attribute and language is our most powerful symbolic system. To develop and understand symbolism and to distinguish reality from fantasy children need to be lucky enough to have adults who will help them. Playing shops can be done by gesture alone or with daisy heads symbolizing money and food. A bumped head may be helped by smacking the 'naughty door that bumped it' but a calm, truthful explanation at another time (a cut knee) will help the child to sort our reality from fantasy and to understand in this case that he is not surrounded by hostile inanimate objects. The ability to think symbolically starts in the pre-school and infant years and continues to develop throughout childhood and adolescence and probably depends on the progressive organization and maturation of the cortex interacting with experience.

Corinne Hutt[11] suggests that imaginative play may provide adults with a 'looking glass in which to glimpse a child's emotional state, his experience and his language competence'. Child guidance clinics admitting children who have experienced a stressful situation and are deeply disturbed have much experience of children repeatedly playing out the situation at the root of its trouble and as a result curing themselves. Close observation of children at play in school under normal conditions may therefore sometimes reveal problems which are often concealed, a knowledge of direct use to teachers who may suggest in what ways they need help. Corinne Hutt's view resembles that of Dr D.W. Winnicott's of many years ago: ' . . . for play, like speech, can be said to be given us to hide out thoughts, if it is the deeper thoughts that we mean'[12].

The answers to the many uncertainties about the role of play and exploration in development will only be discovered by careful observation of children's behaviour. But perhaps it is worth stating here the importance of a young child's needs *each day* rather than fixing on some distant theoretical objective not understood by it and thus to the child of no significance[10]. Play in all its forms may serve a child's needs at the moment and assist development in some yet unknown way. It may assist in the development of the brain model (chapter 10) by influencing the way a child looks at and responds to certain aspects of life. Indeed, rather than avid drilling of the 3 Rs at 4 and 5, play may be the well-spring from which a rich imagination and capacity to experiment develop.

As Maria Montessori[13] wrote perceptively on observation:

> The psychic life of the baby must be observed as Fabre observed his insects, going in search of them to surprise them in their natural environments, and lying hidden so as not to disturb them.

Clearly there is much to be learned about play in all its forms but all *appear to be essential for the intellectual, imaginative and emotional development of the child and may well be necessary steps to a further stage of development.* This is the thirteenth principle.

Habituation

Our basic need for novelty and stimulation is apparent from what I have just said. This allows me to develop another important idea about learning. It seems that the brain can prevent well understood background features from intruding into consciousness, leaving it free to deal with new, important features of the environment. This decrease of the brain in responsiveness to the commonplace is technically called 'habituation'. It is not because the brain has 'forgotten' the continued stimulus. If there is a slight change in its pattern the brain becomes alert to it so that the memory of the older event must have been stored in order for change to be detected. Much of the input into the brain seems to be monitored at an unconscious level with parts of the brain acting as a filter keeping the familiar in the background and selecting the new and interesting for consciousness to deal with.

The capacity to store a memory of an event and therefore to detect change from it happens in the first two or three months of life and seems to be a product of the maturing brain. A baby of six weeks shown a picture of a face repeatedly looks at it just as hard at the fifteenth or sixteenth time of showing as he did at the first. After about eight weeks he becomes bored and soon looks away. He has become 'habituated'. If a checkerboard replaces the face the child's interest increases markedly; a difference must have been noted. So a memory must have been present of the face for the difference to be recognized.

The discovery of habituation may help to resolve some of the many unanswered questions involved in learning. The experiment also provides a basis to commonsense and the experience of teachers and allows the fourteenth principle: *the brain thrives on variety and stimulation. Monotony of surroundings, toys that do only one thing, a classroom display kept up for too long, are soon disregarded by the brain.*

Notes

1 HUTT, C. (1982) 'Towards a taxonomy and conceptual model of play' in DAYE, M.I. (Ed) *Advances in Intrinsic Motivation and Aesthetics* Plenum Press
2 HUTT, C. and HUTT, S.J. (1978) 'Heart rate variability...' in *Human Behaviour and Adaptation*, Reynolds, V. and Jones, M.B., Taylor & Francis
3 SCHILLER, C. (1983) *In His Own Words*, National Association for Primary Education
4 HEIN, A. (1980) 'The development of visually guided behaviour' in HARRIS, C. (Ed) *Visual Coding and Adaptability*, Erlbaum

5 HEIN, R. and HEIN, A. (1963) 'Movement-produced stimulation...' *J. Comp. physiol. psychol.* 56

6 TINBERGEN, N. (1972) 'Functional ethology and the human sciences' *Proc R Soc London B*, 182

7 PASSINGHAM, D. (1982) *The Human Primate*, Freeman

8 TAYLOR, M.M. *et al* (1973) 'Tactual perception of texture' in CORTECUTE, E.C. and FRIEDMAN, M.P. (Eds) *Handbook of Perception* 3, Academic Press

9 WILSON, G. (1986) 'The function of symbolic play in cognitive development'. Unpublished Ph.D. thesis. Keele University

10 HUTT, J. *et al* (1974–79) 'Play, exploration and learning in pre-school children' DES sponsored research

11 YOUNG, J.Z. (1971) *An Introduction to the Study of Man*, Oxford University Press

12 WINNICOTT, D.W. (1969) *The Child, Family and Outside World*, Penguin

13 *The Secret of Childhood* (1936) Longmans

10 Remembering, Learning and Thinking

There are few aspects of school work in which children can make progress without taking careful notice of what they see, hear or otherwise experience and without thinking about their observations[1]. Thoughts depend for their base on what we have learned at first through play and exploration. In turn, learning itself is an extension of memory. Learning, remembering and thinking continually interact from an early age and at the nursery and infant school are gathering force.

I want to attempt to link all three with the storage in the brain cells of a 'model of the world'. This notion is slippery and there are few hard facts to support its physical existence in the brain. The word 'model' at once makes one think of some physical structure that represents the outside world in the head. In whatever form it is, it must lie in the brain cells and be stored in them as a code of some kind.

Central to the working of the model is memory, a property of the nervous system effective in entering and storing information as a code and also recalling it; that is, turning the code into items of past experience which are understood. It will be obvious from everyday experience that our model of the world, our 'experience', is not, and can never be, a static one. Throughout life it is enlarged and

becomes highly personal because of our different individual experiences.

All this is vague and unsatisfactory and empty of fact. What the model is, how it is embodied in the nerve cells and how it works is speculation.

Other organs of the body such as the eye, the heart and kidney are better understood than the brain; and it is helpful in explaining how they work to compare them with machines: the eye with a camera, the heart with a pump, the kidney with a filter. The heart is like a pump and the eye like a camera but the complexity of the brain and its ability to plan ahead and create makes machine analogies hopelessly inadequate.

Memory

Memory, as suggested, is of vital importance to the model. Experience has to be stored somewhere so that new information entering the brain through the senses can be scanned and interpreted against the memory record. Facts are few about how the brain carries this out.

Nevertheless, a mass of work over the past forty or fifty years on animals and by brain surgeons has underlined four important aspects of memory: the critical role of the temporal lobes and hippocampus mentioned in chapters 2 and 8; that many different forms of memory and memory system exist and specific memories are probably stored in the relevant association areas mentioned in chapter 2; that a two-component memory exists, long term and short term; and that the learning of physical skills ('stimulus-response' memory) discussed in chapter 3 seems to have a measure of independence from other forms of memory and learning[2]. I do not want to provide much detail about these aspects of memory but rather to develop them in the context of teaching and learning.

The Mystery of the Hippocampus

Parts of the temporal lobes in both hemispheres are concerned with memory, though some of the left is usually programmed early in life for speech (chapter 7). Memory for words and stories is associated with the left lobe whereas faces, whole patterns, spatial maps and tunes seem to be more significantly associated with the right (chapters 2 and 8). The debate and speculation centres on where the record of these memories is stored and the evidence of the surgeon's knife and of some animal experiments has begun to stiffen speculation with fact and point towards the mysterious sea-horse shaped hippocampus tucked inside each of the temporal lobes. It can be removed on one side of the brain with impunity but if both sides are removed the ability to *activate* the memory thread is lost[3].

Wilder Penfield, the brain surgeon whose discoveries these are, claims that the hippocampi are 'keys of access' to the records of particular events ('event' memory) but it seems that it is the cortex that interprets and presents them to 'consciousness'. Penfield's records of patients' memory flashbacks ('events'), stimulated by a gentle electrical current from an electrode applied to the open brain, are mentioned on page 14.

The important point for us is that in normal life we are not subjected to electrodes while the record cannot be voluntarily reactivated otherwise our brain would be jammed with a confusion of memories. Other, at present mysterious, brain mechanisms must act as a kick-start to activate a stream of memories with amazing promptness and accuracy for the specific purpose of comparing present information (this situation in front of us now) with a stream of relevant past events so that action can be taken in the light of past experience. I will pick up this last point in a moment but it should be noted that even though both

hippocampi are removed, a fair memory of the distant past remains.

This fact underlines the important point made earlier that memory is a basic property of the brain and is not restricted to one bit of it. The 'event' memories described by Penfield might have their base in the hippocampi and also in areas of the temporal and frontal cortex.

Abstract Memory

The widespread and dynamic nature of memory in the brain is further underlined by our abstract memory which in a way represents our general store of knowledge. Abstract memory seems to preserve the meaning of objects separated from the particular, detailed memories of the events (the 'event' memory described by Penfield). Concepts — texture, colour, form, size, shape, weight, volume — transformed from a series of sharp experiences such as those provided daily in the classrooms, are possibly embodied all through the association areas of the cortex. Damage to these areas interferes with our abstract memory.

Computer Not Slot Machine

In day to day life at home, on the streets and in the class-room a child draws on his memory to think and decide. To build up his abstract memory his event memory needs feeding at school with particular, concrete experiences so that concepts such as weight and colour are built up soundly out of first-hand knowledge. All this is done through a range of work which begins pre-school and starts to 'ground' in the infant years.

But how might a child (or adult) use his memory to think and decide? One theory is that before a decision is reached and action taken the brain works towards an answer by running through a sequence of operations something like the situation that now confronts it, rather like a film played back (event memory). So that when a dog runs to greet a child his brain mechanism flashes a patterned nerve message of this dog now from the visual parts of the brain to the memory systems. Memories of other dogs are recalled and scanned. The brain compares the two images: this dog now running to greet the child and memories of other dogs and sees a similarity. If the child has previously been bitten then he will be cautious. As he grows more and more used to dogs, most of which are friendly, his memory tells him that he may reach down to pat it.

A child must not learn too quickly or he will begin to link things which have only come together by chance. He must wait for the association to be repeated. As the repetitions grow more frequent, his behaviour (towards dogs) becomes increasingly more confident. A child must be capable of unlearning so that if conditions change his brain does not remain fixed in a wrong response. All this points to the nerve cells of the cortex operating to detect associations, or what Phillips and others have called 'suspicious coincidences'[4]. This allows the brain to estimate rapidly the relative probabilities of possible alternatives so that in one set of circumstances one response to a stimulus is appropriate whereas in another set of circumstances a different response to the same stimulus is required. In other words the brain is like a computer and not a slot machine, which keeps count of the number of occurrences of events so that *statistically* it knows the chances of situation B following A rather than C.

So the brain must not learn or unlearn to quickly or like a weathercock it will spin, a prey to every changing wind. A child of 3, provided that he knows where mother is and has good reason to believe that she will come back, soon begins to accept another fairly familiar person even when he is not in a too familiar place. He can talk with his mother and understand her message: 'Back later'. He will remember that this has happened before and everything will be alright. His mother will have brought him to school or playgroup and stayed with him the first time or two while he explored near her. His memory says the situation is reasonable. He feels secure. But she must be back or he will lose confidence as the memory systems begin to give way to uncertainty.

Through language, play, imitation, exploration, books and instruction our event and abstract memory enlarges and the model of the world inside the head grows and refines. Each time a child learns something there must be changes in his brain but what they involve is at present unknown.

Memory and Learning

I suggested earlier that we can only speculate about the physical nature of the model but whatever it is it must lie in the cells of the brain. The enormous task before brain science is to demonstrate the nature of the change in the brain cells that establishes a memory record and to show how this stored record is turned into scenes as fresh and bright as when first recorded or into voices heard long ago. Nevertheless despite precise evidence a fifteenth general principle may be stated: *that the whole purpose of teaching and learning is to develop a model which is knowledge-based and flexible enough to cope with the situations that a person is likely to meet with.*

Where is the memory record out of which the model is built and in what form is it held? One belief, no more, is that memory depends on changed connections between nerves. These synaptic connections are so numerous that looking for changes before and after learning is like looking for a needle in a haystack. Another speculation is that the memory record is stored in specific chemical molecules. What they are and how they would break down to yield memories and then reform to be used again is unclear. There are no signs of such molecules from brain experiments.

Despite these complexities six aspects of memory will be recognized from day-to-day experience. First, is Jerome Bruner's[5] axiom which states that *the most basic thing that can be said about human memory after a century of intensive research is that detail must be placed into a structured pattern or it will rapidly forgotten.* This is my sixteenth principle. If the material lacks structure a child will remember much less than if the material is connected up into a pattern as in a story or sentence. In doing this the brain is exercising its normal protective functions which are not to remember things that do not belong to a pattern and to filter out the irrelevant. To remember everything would be an embarrassment.

Chapter 7 described how the brain might analyze patterns of sound into speech. It is abundantly clear that the search for pattern by the human brain is a fundamental tendency probably programmed by heredity. A young child is not haphazard, for example, in scanning the environment. He seems to search naturally for combinations of features which give clues to their nature and function. For example, there is a very early response to faces. As remarked on in chapter 7, it appears to be a basic function of the nervous system to analyze these patterns in order to detect similarity among differences. So, when a young child paints, his picture of 'Mummy' will follow a lawful pattern. The units or parts of a painting are related to one another in a sequence and the sequences change with age. Children usually move from top to bottom and left to right. Mummy is usually painted by a 3-year-old as a circle with some face details, then legs. Some stop there leaving armless figures. Others 'go back to finish', to add arms, ears, hair and so on. This suggests that the child has become adept at monitoring; at running an eye over a piece of work to see if all the pieces are present, thus reinforcing the notion that the brain is searching for a pattern. The brain may indeed search for 'linking features' to make sense of an object — for example, two colinear lines belonging to a particular shape even if widely separated in the image — 'in much the same way, when trying to solve a jig-saw puzzle, one looks for "blue sky" or "brickwork" or "foliage" in order to narrow the search for matching pieces'[6].

Left to himself a young child will seldom tire of making all-over patterns or patterned borders in paint or crayon round a story. To strengthen this natural tendency a teacher should seek to help a young child or older pupil to look for significant patterns in data or other information and offer explanations for them[7]. Opportunities for discriminating, classifying, observing and generalising from interrelations arise in connection with work in all areas of the curriculum — reading, mathematics, art, craft, science — and in day to day activities such as laying the table for dinner, positioning the chairs in a classroom and arranging flowers but they could be used more fully than they are at present.

Second, and continuing with pattern, spelling does not appear to be a hearing skill (deaf children are better spellers than peers of the same reading age) but a visual skill and also a kind of grammar. Sight is our preferred sense and we rely on looking to check almost everything we do. This is true of spelling. The fact that vision plays a big part in spelling is shown by the large number of poor spellers that have some visual defect.

As in word sequences, there is a scale of probability from letters that can occur in sequence to those that cannot occur (for example, the initial H will not be followed by another consonant). *The secret of learning to spell appears to be linked to the ability to absorb letter patterns* and this is the seventeenth principle. Dr Margaret Peters[8], whose ideas these are, suggests that words should always be written out for a child, never spelled out. The child should then follow the 'look, cover, write, check' routine: look at the word first, cover it up, write it out from memory and then check that it is right. By doing this the word is imprinted on the child's visual memory.

Third, and my eighteenth principle, *a child remembers only those things to which he pays keen attention. None of the things he ignores appears to leave a memory trace in the brain*[3]. Only when a child is focussing the spotlight of his attention on something that really interests him, or more to the point, something that is made interesting and relevant, is it likely to be recorded in the brain cells. Each time a baby or older child explores, each time he directs his attention stubbornly onto something, the brain cells are being changed and the child is learning.

Fourth, memory seems to be impaired by anxiety[9]. All of us suffer from anxiety from time to time but anxiety about home conditions may cause some children to refuse school. These children are not primarily frightened of school but feel some insecurity at home. They think, sometimes correctly that their parents may abandon them if they let them out of sight, or may drop dead or be unbearably lonely while they are away at school. One effect of all these anxieties is to impair concentration and memory. Knowledge and understanding of home circumstances are essential to help a child over his difficulties.

Fifth, human memory and learning thrive on associations. Say a word — 'mother' for instance — and at once a collection of memories and associations are summoned up, different for each person. A baby associates the mother's face with a collection of other associated memories — food, warmth, pleasure, songs — which must be built into the manifold nerve webs in the brain. Another child, deprived in some way, may build up other different associations that may distort and cramp his particular model of mother.

Sixth, most of us are aware of two kinds of memory, long and short term. We use short term memory to hold a telephone number between directory and dial, furiously repeating it lest we forget it, though if anyone interrupts us we forget it very rapidly. Indeed after a few seconds or minutes this kind of information evaporates. It perhaps is a 'working memory', something held in the forefront of the mind while we are attending to something. In reading (chapter 8) 'it is where you lodge the traces of what you have just read while you go on to make sense of the next few words'[10].

Long-term memory is distinguished from the short-term by its enduring character, even for much of a long lifetime. Old people, as we know, can retain and recall childhood memories vividly — for example their first day at school — but somehow fail to enter new memories. This constant, permanent memory can survive when the brain has been cooled or has been in coma or under anaesthetic. Such memory must have as a basis some enduring change which is built into the fine structure of the nervous system.

Memory is probably the central question of brain function yet we have no firm evidence of its physical structure or how it works. If we did it would illuminate teaching considerably.

Sleep

Sleep is the other side of learning. Children are very variable in the amount of sleep they need. The average total sleep time of a newborn baby is around sixteen-and-a-half hours but the range of variation lies between ten-and-a-half and twenty-three hours.

These variations are quite normal. With age there is a gradual decline in sleep time so that by three weeks the average is about fourteen-and-a-half hours. Some older children sleep long, some short hours. It is very likely that these individual differences are present from birth and are inherited.

The function of sleep is strangely controversial. It is

certainly complex and different patterns of electrical brain waves are associated with different patterns of sleep experienced in a normal night. Rapid eye movement (REM) sleep (where the eyelids and eyes move in sleep) is linked with dreaming and vigorous body movement. The brain waves are like waking waves (rapid) and are associated with an increased rate of cell firing in many parts of the brain. A theory, no more, is that children take more REM sleep during periods of rapid learning, perhaps when memory input and coding are great. Deep sleep is associated with large, slow waves and a lower rate of firing.

On commonsense grounds, sleep gives the brain 'the rest it deserves'. Perhaps some nerve cells in the brain which are the seat of immense activity during the day and where chemical changes go on, need to recover. The average rate of cell firing certainly declines in sleep. So sleep may be a period of maintenance and repair of the nerve cell networks used in memory, problem solving and learning.

It is perhaps significant that so much time is spent in sleep by infants and young children when presumably many new synapses are being formed in the brain and the intellect is growing fast (chapter 5). A child is learning very early on in life to integrate information from eye, muscle, joint and skin when he explores in order to provide himself with a valid model of the world, as explained in chapters 4 and 9. At nursery and infant school exploration continues but at infant school especially learning is swift (chapter 1). The sheer effort devoted to learning during the period from birth to 8 is likely to be greater than at any other period in life. As we grow old our speed of learning diminishes and the need for the slow processes of recovery during sleep is also reduced.

I mentioned a moment ago that structural changes in laying down a memory record might take place at synapses. Learning in fact might alter them. If this is so, Moruzzi[11] suggests that a distinction should be made between synapses that 'learn' and those concerned with routine tasks of transmitting impulses along inborn pathways. These synapses may need no sleep. Those of the nerve cells of the spinal cord and of the bulb (chapter 2) belong to this category. Sleep perhaps is mainly to permit 'recovery' of the learning synapses in the association and motor areas of the cortex and cerebellum. If this is so at the end of a long period of learning if we could see the synapses in the cortex we should perhaps be 'more impressed by the ruins than by new construction'[11].

These are speculations but commonsense and experience tell us that sleeping on a problem helps to clarify and consolidate thoughts and can be calming. *For practical purposes a child is not getting enough sleep if he seems tired the next day. A tired child cannot play, explore and learn properly.* This is my nineteenth principle.

Notes

1 *Primary Education in England* (1978) HMSO
2 NEWCOMBE, F. (1980) 'Memory: A neuropsychological approach', *TINS*, 3.
3 PENFIELD, W. and ROBERTS, L. (1959) *Speech and Brain Mechanisms*, Princeton
4 PHILLIPS, C.G. *et al.* (1984) 'Localisation of function in the cerebral cortex', *Brain*, 107
5 BRUNER, J. (1960) *The Process of Education*, Harvard.
6 BARLOW, H.B. (1985) 'The role of single neurons ...', *Quarterly Journal of Experimental Psychology*, 37A.
7 Department of Education and Science (1985) *The Curriculum from 5–16*, HMSO
8 PETERS, M. (1967) *Spelling: Caught or Taught*, Routledge & Kegan Paul.
9 BOWLBY, J. (1973) *Separation: Anxiety and Anger*, Hogarth
10 SMITH, F. (1978) *Understanding Reading*, Holt

11 MORUZZI, G. (1965) 'The functional significance of sleep with particular regard to the mechanisms underlying consciousness', in ECCLES, J.C. (Ed) *Brain and Conscious Experience*, Springer-Verlag.

11   *What We Are Born With*

It is only necessary to look round a class of children or at your family to see how people differ. It is not only obvious physically in hair, height or eye colour but in ability and behaviour too.

In a class of 5-year-olds some have excellent hand control, can cut out with scissors, draw straight lines and circles, while others are clumsy. Some are shy, others bold. Among older children every teacher knows the child who needs pushing and the other who needs freedom and will use it.

Basic Genetics

What is at the bottom of these commonplace observations? How much is due to what the individual is 'born with' and how much depends on upbringing? Lord Chesterfield's view of the matter, as expressed in a letter to his son aged 15 in 1784 was, 'that people are, in general, what they are made, by education and company, from fifteen to twenty-five; consider well, therefore, the importance of your next eight or nine years — your whole future depends on them'. We may hope that Lord Chesterfield would have modified his structures in the light of what is known about human development today.

We now know that the differences between people come from many sources. Broadly speaking they are divided into those that are hereditary or genetic on the one hand and those that are due to the environment on the other. This is not a simple clear-cut matter because heredity and environment interact in the production of each and every character and we cannot say how much has been contributed by either for most human characteristics. The proportion of the inherited to the environmental component is unique to each individual. This is because each one of us has been formed by a sort of genetic lottery and is but one of a vast number of 'possible children' any one of whom might have been conceived and born if a different sperm with its unique arrangements had chance to fertilize the mother's egg cell, likewise with its unique gene arrangements.

Let us look briefly at the origins of human individuality. The natural (genetic) uniqueness is due basically to the shuffling of the chromosome sets during gamete formation and the rearrangement of the determinants (genes) carried by them so that each egg or sperm which carries one half set of twenty-three chromosomes is unique. The seal is set upon individual uniqueness at the moment of fertilization when the double set of forty-six chromosomes is reformed. From this fertilized egg every cell in the body, wherever located, is developed by repeated division so that in each cell is the unique double set of chromosomes (for the chromosome basis of sex differences see chapter 8).

Is it possible to make an estimate of the relative importance of heredity and environment? Yes, to some extent by making use of studies on twins and a while range of other observations.

One-egg or identical twins are formed from the splitting of a single fertilized egg and thus have a common hereditary endowment. They are, in a way, duplicate human beings

having identical genes and thus starting with the same potentialities. Identical twins can be used to estimate the differences that arise mainly from the environment because their
differences must arise largely from the differences in the
environment around each twin and the things that happen to
it. Even before birth their different positions in the uterus
put them in special environments from the outset. Identical
twins may sometimes be reared apart in very different home
environments as happens when they are orphaned and separated at birth; yet despite this they are remarkably similar in
IQ.

Two-egg twins (not identical) have quite different
gene outfits since each egg has been fertilized by a different
sperm. They are, in fact, no more alike than brother and
sister except that they have shared a common uterine environment for nine months. They can be used to show the
shades and types of genetic differences which arise within a
family since the family environment is essentially the same
for both.

If the IQ of separated identical twins is measured it
has, in statistical jargon, a correlation coefficient of about
0.87 compared with a coefficient of 0.45 for non-identical
twins brought up together. A correlation of 1.0 would
mean identical in intelligence, and nought, complete lack of
identity.

On the twin evidence heredity does seem to have a large
share in IQ measurements. If, for instance, we went into a
playground and picked out at random a few children of the
same sex and age the average difference between their IQs
would be about seventeen points; with non-identical twins
reared together, twelve points; with identical twins reared
apart, six points. The environment then does not seem to
affect general basic intelligence a great deal. Other evidence
from twins suggests that home influences such as how much
a child is talked to and read to and reads to himself affects
reading and spelling ability but arithmetical ability seems to

be more determined by native wit and not so much by environment[1].

Heredity-environment Interaction

Earlier in this chapter I mentioned the difficulties of disentangling the contribution of heredity and environment in most characters. Just how difficult this is in humans is shown by a study of the causes of weight variation in babies at birth[2]. Thirty per cent of the variation is due to unknown causes. The rest have been categorized thus: the influence of the hereditary constitution of the mother (20 per cent), of the child (16 per cent), and the sex of the child (2 per cent). Of environmental influences, 24 per cent of the weight variation is due to the mother's health and nutrition, 7 per cent to the order of the baby's birth and 1 per cent to the mother's age. Of course, it would be remarkable if all the differences between human beings could be strictly determined but it is important to understand more of the reasons behind the differences, especially of behaviour, if we are to plan the context for teaching and learning better.

Heritability and Education

Physical variation was mentioned in the first paragraph of this chapter and of this variation in height is a striking feature though in rather older children (13–14) than we are concerned with here. In England, height variation is largely due to inherited factors because children usually get enough to eat and are seldom stunted by preventable disease. In poorer parts of the world where food is short and doctors scarce a greater proportion of the variation will be due to environmental causes. This simple example drives home the nonsense of the idea of fixed characteristics as due to '80 per cent heredity and 20 per cent environment' as a blanket statement. It allows the development of three ideas important for education.

First, the notion of heritability of characteristics[3]. The proportion of the variation of a trait in a population assignable to genetic causes is called the heritability of the character. Heritability says nothing about the inheritance of a trait between particular parents and their offspring but refers only to the population. Estimates of the heritability of height or intelligence are rated only for the population from which they have been obtained. They are not valid for future populations or for such new environments as could be produced by new school or housing policies. The technical measure of heritability is a number between nought and 1.0 which states how much of the variation of a trait is due to genetic variation. To take a specific case; a value of 0.5 is calculated to be the inherited contribution to variation in IQ over much of the population of America and Western Europe at the present time and for the last fifty years. This value is based on evidence drawn almost entirely from whites and thus it can be said that about half of the variation in IQ in whites is due to the genes. It is impossible to use these proportions for other countries or peoples.

Group differences can be very disturbing in their implications for different ethnic and social groups but when the criterion is concerned with people's brain power a particularly sensitive area is entered because most people mind very much about their ability. Comparison of the IQ of groups brings out average differences and their magnitude and as a result specific questions can be asked about such differences. Programmes can then be devised that concentrate and compensate for group handicap. Concentration on average differences should not, however, divert attention away from the individual. The individual in terms of his actual performance should be the proper unit of our concern. It is he who must learn. Dr Johnson put it very plainly about a specific and important group difference. 'Which have the most brains, men or women?', he was asked; his reply, 'Which man, Sir, which woman?'

Second, the more uniform the environment the greater will be the importance of genetic variation. In other words the more uniform the education system the more sharply the genetic differences in intelligence will be revealed between individuals. The ordinary person will be cleverer if the environment for the majority is improved in a blanket sense but intelligence running in families (both high and low) will be seen more obviously.

Clearly 'uniformity' of environment is a somewhat theoretical notion since each school, whatever its character, is bound to be unique because of the individuals who teach and learn in it. But insufficiently differentiated schemes of work or teaching materials which aims at the middle of the class or whole-class teaching are common tendencies in the direction of blanket treatment. In these circumstances equalization and a lowering of standards and a beating down to a common mediocrity, talent and energy are the general effects, not optimization of abilities and raising general standards.

Thus, the more diverse the opportunities made by tailoring environments according to the needs of individuals the more the level of achievement and success of the population as a whole will be raised, for this policy optimizes the environment for everybody. In this situation no environment will be 'better' than any other. Each and every individual because of his different (not 'better') hereditary make-up requires a different environment if he or she is to develop his or her major skills to the utmost. This is a far-off goal to aim for because it is complex but it is one worth striving for. Many primary schools attempt successfully to create a unique environment for each child and have done so for many years by a judicious mixture of whole class, group and individual teaching. But different treatments for all as far as the system allows is just treatment for all while equal treatment is not, a policy which applies equally to the least and the most able.

Intelligence and IQ Tests

From what has been said about heritability it is likely that about half of the IQ differences among individuals that make up a population is accounted for by genes and the rest by environmental influences. The actual proportion does not matter, what is important is the relevance of genetics to mental ability. This is not to say that education cannot change mental qualities. The plasticity of the young brain, within limits, shows that it is possible. One of the many functions of a school is to spot and develop inborn potential but no matter how good it is at this it is impossible to make a nuclear physicist out of a child with a low IQ. As all good teachers know, however, success needs to be found for each and every child.

This is not the place to go into detail about intelligence tests but it is important to know how reliable and how stable they are. If the child's IQ is 100 at age 10 will it go on being that for the rest of life?

If the test is properly standardized, that is, tested on large numbers of children chosen at random, it is repeatable; that is, the same pattern of scores will emerge on a retest. Because the sample is random many children will be grouped in the middle (children of average IQ) and fewer will appear at the extremes, that is, subnormal and highly intelligent children. It follows that the standardisation will be better and the test more repeatable for the most numerous (the 'average' of IQ about 90–110) than for children outside these ranges and especially the few at the extremes. In practice it means that a test may be given to a bright child one day and he may score 145, on another 140. Mistakes do occur and if parents and teachers do not believe the result of a test they should say so and the matter can be looked into: emotional upset, anxiety, insufficient interest in school work, ill health, poor sight and slight deafness can all affect the result.

A few points about testing procedures might be worth making here. First, that 'intelligence' as measured by tests is only a relative quality dependent very much on the place, time and culture as I emphasized earlier. It is an abstraction and if we give it meaning more than a mere relationship we do so at our peril. We can say nothing about an individual's measured IQ except in relation to that of other individuals in a population.

Second, intelligence cannot be isolated from other facets of human behaviour[4]. Intelligent activity, the ability to grasp the essentials of a situation and respond appropriately to them is affected by mood, attitude, temperament, character or aspiration. In other words thinking and feeling cannot easily be separated. Low expectation of teachers and feckless parents can breed low standards of attainment.

Third, IQ has been 'defined' rather narrowly on the quality measured by the highly fallible instrument of intelligence tests. We all know pretty well what we mean by intelligence. Many would agree with Cyril Burt's definition[5]. He called it, 'innate, general, cognitive ability', innate because it has a big inherited component, general because it enters into every form of mental ability and cognitive because it is an intellectual quality, that is it involves knowing rather than feeling.

There are some obvious weakneses in this broad definition. People have fingerprint individuality and if we are to allow individuals to develop optimally, differences must be recognized and encouraged. While a broad and balanced curriculum should be fostered at school the strengths of individuals should also be developed. There are brilliant musicians and gifted painters with an IQ of about 90. There are many children whose minds a teacher may envy who turn out to have moderate IQs but have flair in design, experimental work or literature. In this regard the assessment of a careful, observant teacher adds a vital dimension to an IQ score but the two assessments should be complementary and not competitive. But for giftedness to be revealed the work set should stimulate ingenuity and originality. Art materials tend to be used generally to make pictures but three-dimensional work using a variety of materials — wood, clay, polystyrene, cardboard, string and so on — will reveal other talents. For children to show other strengths, in written work, for example, a good range of stimuli are necessary — stories, music, science experiments. Of course, such provision will stimulate individual enterprise in all children, not only the gifted, and should be there for them.

Fourth, to rub in the point about individuality and learning, a child's personality may have a considerable effect on how he learns and how 'intelligent' he appears. Extroverted children do better when rules are given after practice but introverted children do better when rules are given before. Extroverted children prefer instruction by the teacher to instruction by machine and do better this way, while introverted children show the opposite effect.[6] Of practical significance for the classroom, 'discovery' methods applied thoughtlessly to all children may put some at a grave disadvantage.

IQ Stability

As for stability of IQ, from the age of about 7 or 8 IQ does not change much for the majority and after ten it is pretty well stable until senescence[3]. Stability does not, however, imply fixed rigidity. In some 10 per cent of children changes of 30 IQ points over the junior and later school years are found. In the majority of children changes of 1–10 IQ points are commonplace. These small changes do not reflect real changes in intellectual capacities. Aggressive, independent and competitive children, children from homes with books about and plenty of interesting conversation are more likely to show upward movements in IQ than other children; and boys gain on average more than girls. For practical purposes we should be sceptical about ascribing too high a reliability to a single IQ test in early childhood. Like the results of medical examinations, IQ test results date and need a periodic review to establish whether significant changes have taken place; and like medical inspections they need planned action afterwards.

The Gene Outfit and Intelligence

How do we know that the genetic outfit of an individual is important in determining intelligence? The early part of this chapter gave some evidence but two points are worth developing.

First, that exceptionally a genius or very gifted child is born to unexceptional parents (or vice versa). This is because he has inherited an arrangement of genes which on the basis of the chance mixing of parental genes is extremely improbable. Genius is a chancy quality because the children or brothers or sisters of geniuses are not always exceptional themselves. In the children of a genius the star quality may lose its brightness because when the genius reproduces, his unique gene outfit is dismantled in reproduction and new ones are built up with the mother's (or father's) genes. It is unlikely that the precise gene arrangements that gave the particular genius star quality will turn up again.

On a more ordinary level, witness the commonplace conflicts that arise between parent and child. Even though that child has a better chance of being like his parents than anyone else in the world, the genetic individuality of the child overrides the parental environment. Heredity is grittier than this.

Second, and perhaps the most important evidence that heredity plays a substantial role in intellectual performance, is that new facts can be predicted from the genetical theory. The genetical theory of inheritance can be used to say that such and such might be the result by forecasting the results of observations or experiment. In other words the theory does not merely account for the facts of inheritance but anticipates the unknown. Thus the difference between the IQs of one-egg and two-egg twins can be predicted by the genetical theory of inheritance, since two-egg twins, like brothers and sisters, have only half their genes in common on average while one-egg twins have identical gene outfits.

Where does all this get us to? The uniqueness of the individual is the product of an interaction between heredity and environment. Each of us inherits a genetic outfit that endows us with certain potentialities which may or may not be fulfilled as we grow up but the genes set a limit to what each of us can in the best circumstances achieve. The human brain as shown has a wide margin of flexibility for the environment to have its effect on. IQ scores are a useful but rough pointer to potential ability and they should not be treated as infallible predictors. They were not, in any case, designed to test contemporary modular theories of brain organization.

All neat and tidy systems of classification are wrong; human nature would not fit into them. The biological evidence suggests that we need the most flexible organization that we can manage so that we can maximize individual abilities. But organization is merely a framework in which children should find it possible to produce their best work. We do our best to release the powers of each pupil by providing in this framework individual attention and particular methods, approaches and resources, that is a 'special' environment. This is an ideal aim because there are as many human natures as there are individuals and time is precious. Compromise is necessary between individual attention in a class, small group work and whole class teaching arranged according to what is being taught and the needs of the children. At a later stage, streaming and setting children of roughly similar abilities will be necessary. In the nursery school/class, play, exploration and practical activities form the basis of the work and individual and group work obtain. The twentieth principle follows: *that it is just to treat different persons differently so long as each is treated as well as possible[7].*

In this chapter I have been much concerned with IQ and tests. They have their uses in a rough and ready way though they tell us little about the fine grain of the mind. It is worth quoting Binet's[8] (1908) original notion of 'intelligence' (he after all invented the famous IQ test). It sums up the wonderful variability and potential of people which are the strengths of society and Binet's own words form the final principle of this book.

> *Our examination of intelligence cannot take account of all those qualities — attention, will, popularity, perseverance, teachableness and courage which play so important a part in school work, and also in after life; for life is not so much a conflict of intelligence as a struggle between characters.*

Notes

1 BURT, C. (1966) 'The genetic determination of differences in intelligence . . .', *British Journal of Psychology*, 57
2 PENROSE, L.S. (1963) *Outline of Human Genetics*, Heinemann

3 HERRNSTEIN, R.J. (1973) *IQ in the Meritocracy*, Allen Lane

4 HEIM, A. (1970) *Intelligence and Personality*, Pelican

5 BURT, C. (1962) *Mental and Scholastic Tests*, Staples

6 EYSENCK, H.J. (1975) *Equality and Education: fact and fiction*

7 THODAY, J.M. (1965) 'Geneticism and Environmentalism', in *Biological Aspects of Social Problems*, Oliver and Boyd

8 BINET, A. (1908) *L'anee psychologique*, but quoted in Department of Education and Science *The Hadow Report*, HMSO

12 The Twenty-one Principles

1 Most of the cortex at birth is like a blank slate on which the lessons of experience will be written, including those of language. The nature of the slate is, of course, determined by heredity (chapter 2, page 17).

2 What is well and soundly grounded in young children is likely to remain with them (chapter 3, page 23).

3 The years from birth to puberty are a crucial time when the ability to learn is at flood readiness (chapter 5, page 29).

4 Although in general we appear to pay a price for the plasticity of the young human cortex, great benefits can be bestowed through teaching because of this early adaptive plasticity. It is crucial to detect visual and auditory handicaps early, at two or earlier if possible, for this allows advice and treatment to be given while the chances of improvement are high (chapter 6, page 34).

5 Brain growth is bound up with body growth and the promotion of the best general body growth possible in the period before the second or third birthday is the most that can be done to ensure good brain growth (chapter 6, page 37).

6 It is the compounding of poor circumstances including those in pregnancy that conspire to harm the brain and

intellect rather than the critical influence of the early childhood years in their own right (chapter 6, page 40).

7 The brain in scanning the environment, whether for sight, sound or touch, is not haphazard but searches for clues to pattern. For teaching and learning related knowledge is powerful to understanding and is remembered (chapter 7, page 53).

8 The brain is poised at birth to learn speech (chapter 7, page 53).

9 Man has developed a great capacity for imitation and the most powerful of all didactic tools is the exemplar of parents and teachers (Chapter 8, page 61).

10 More numerical, experimental and spatial activities should be stage-managed for girls so that they will learn through manipulation and experiment as well as through talk (chapter 8, page 63).

11 It is prudent to plan to make full use of the strengths of both hemispheres. By exercising the rather underused right hemisphere the performance of both might be improved (chapter 8, page 68).

12 A child does not learn from a passive kaleidoscope of experiences but from the outcomes of actions that he or she has initiated (chapter 9, page 75).

13 All forms of play appear to be essential for the intellectual, imaginative and emotional development of the child and may well be necessary steps to a further stage of development (chapter 9, page 81).

14 The brain thrives on variety and stimulation. Monotony of surroundings, toys that do only one thing, a classroom display kept up for too long, are soon disregarded by the brain (chapter 9, page 82).

15 The whole purpose of teaching and learning is to develop a brain 'model' which is knowledge-based and flexible enough to cope with the situations that a person is likely to meet with (chapter 10, page 89).

16 The most basic thing that can be said about human

memory after a century of intensive research is that detail must be placed into a structured pattern or it will be rapidly forgotten (chapter 10, page 90).

17 The secret of learning to spell is linked to the ability to absorb letter patterns (chapter 10, page 91).

18 A child remembers only those things to which he pays keen attention. None of the things he ignores appears to leave a memory trace in the brain (chapter 10, page 92).

19 A child is not getting enough sleep if he seems tired the next day. A tired child cannot play, explore and learn properly (chapter 10, page 95).

20 It is just to treat different persons differently so long as each is treated as well as possible (chapter 11, page 108).

21 'Our examination of intelligence cannot take account of all those qualities — attention, will, popularity, perseverance, teachableness and courage which play so important a part in school work, and also in after life; for life is not so much a conflict of intelligence as a struggle between characters' (chapter 11, page 108).

13 Conclusions

It will be obvious from this book that the brain which guides our lives is fiendishly complex. Although substantial progress has been made in understanding some parts of the brain as one layer of complexity is penetrated another is revealed which prevents an overall understanding of its function. How we think, memorize a poem, do a sum, read or write a letter, is nowhere near understood in terms of brain function. To add a final complicating observation or two; it seems that some neuronal machinery (the synapse ?), as chapter 10 indicated, makes us retain all that rivets our attention as a 'memory trace'. Amazingly all this goes on against a much larger 'background' activity of neurones which has nothing to do with the specific memory. Moruzzi[1] puzzling over this over twenty years ago concluded that, 'all these considerations lead to the conclusion that the neural processes underlying learning and forgetting, storage and retrieval of memory traces are quantitatively small with respect to the background activity of the cerebrum, although the highest achievements of mankind, from artistic creation to scientific discovery, are dependent upon them'.

Twenty years on, the unravelling of these specific processes still seems a distant prospect. Once a clear theoretical structure emerges about how the brain works the effect will be like a roman candle illuminating the barren territory of education theory. Despite this complexity enough has been discovered now for me to have had the temerity to suggest twenty-one broad principles arising largely from brain studies for teaching and learning. Although mainly general in nature they provide insight into brain function and abundant support for the day-to-day practice, commonsense and instincts of the vast majority of parents and teachers. To be able to do this today is to salute the courage, persistence and brilliance of those who attempt to understand and explain the workings of this mysterious organ.

Note

1 MORUZZI, G. (1965) 'The functional significance of sleep with particular regard to the mechanisms underlying consciousness', in *Brain and Conscious Experience*, Eccles, J.C. (Ed.) Springer-Verlag

Some Useful Books on the Human Brain

Blakemore, Colin   *Mechanics of the Mind*, CUP (1977)

Brierley, John   *The Thinking Machine* Heinemann (1973)

Brierley, John   *The Growing Brain*, NFER (1976)

Elliot, H.C.   *The Shape of Intelligence*, Allen and Unwin (1970)

Frisby, J.P.   *Seeing*, OUP (1979)

Laslett, P. (Ed.)   *The Physical Basis of Mind*, Blackwell (1950)

Penfield, Wilder   *The Mystery of the Mind*, Princeton (1975)

Penfield, Wilder and Roberts, L.   *Speech and Brain Mechanisms*, Princeton (1959)

Young, J.Z.   *Programs of the Brain*, OUP (1978)

Index